Teaching Students To Get Along ™

Lee Canter and Katia Petersen

D1314204

A Publication of Lee Canter & Associates

Contributing Writers
Nancy Hereford
Carol Provisor

Editors
Marlene Canter
Jacqui Hook
Phyllis Lerner
Steven Petersen
Barbara Schadlow
Kathy Winberry

Design
Carol Provisor

©1995 Lee Canter & Associates
P.O. Box 2113, Santa Monica, CA 90407-2113
800-262-4347   310-395-3221

Printed in the United States of America
First Printing May 1995
99 98 97 96   8 7 6 5 4 3

Library of Congress Catalog Card Number 95-69590
ISBN 0-939007-99-1

Contents

Forward

We live in a world where tempers seem to grow shorter all the time. There's less caring and consideration for others; more anger, more violence. Some people say there's little we can do about these problems, that there's little we can do to counteract the violence that children see on television, in the streets, in their own homes. From years of working with dedicated teachers and educators nationwide, I know that's not true.

One educator whose story was most convincing to me is Katia Petersen, who has joined with me in writing this resource book and in developing the graduate course on which it's based. War taught Katia profound lessons about the necessity of teaching children to get along.

Katia was 16 years old and living in her native Cyprus when fighting broke out between Greece and Turkey over her homeland. She remembers being terrified by the bombing, by the soldiers, by the terrible devastation. But in the midst of that chaos, a Red Cross worker asked her to help supervise a group of orphaned children. In that shelter, with bombs falling outside, she discovered that even under the worst circumstances imaginable, she could give hope to children. As she spun stories about life in another world, a more peaceful world, where people were kind and cared about one another, she could see that those frightened children were with her. As Katia describes it, "The children were using their imaginations to create a better world than the one they were in. Despite the pain and suffering they had experienced, they could imagine a place where people were able to get along."

Right then, says Katia, she knew she wanted to spend her life helping children learn that there are better ways to respond to conflict than by fighting and hurting others. She wanted to help other adults learn how to tap the well of strength and resiliency in children that can enable them to overcome the worst and still grow into healthy, caring adults. The strategies you will learn in this book are based on those both Katia and I have developed to help students get along.

There may not be bombs falling where you live, but chances are you're witnessing in ways big or small the physical and emotional devastation of the epidemic of violence in children's lives. That's what has brought you to this book. That's why you're looking for help in teaching students to get along.

You'll find plenty of ideas and guidance here. But what you *won't* find is a formula or a quick fix. Teaching students to get along isn't about presenting an occasional lesson on manners or respect. Reading this book and teaching the lessons contained in it are just the start. To truly be successful in helping students learn to get along with others and respond to conflict in peaceful ways, you have to make teaching and reinforcing prosocial skills as important in your classroom as teaching reading or math or social studies or science. You have to believe in the value of teaching students to get along and capitalize on every opportunity to do so. You have to model cooperation and caring in your own interactions with students, parents, and colleagues.

And trust me, it's not as hard or as much work as it may sound. But it requires a shift in how you think about your role as a teacher and about the role of schooling in general. It requires giving up the assumption that it's not a teacher's job to teach social skills—that you're about teaching reading and math, not teamwork or taking turns.

You are about teaching all of those skills and more, because you're about teaching *children*.

You *can* teach students to get along. Katia and I will show you how.

About the Authors

Lee Canter, who resides in Los Angeles, California, is a recognized national authority on education and child behavior management. Today, just as in 1976 when he cofounded his company with his wife, Marlene Canter, Mr. Canter believes that his primary mission is to provide educators with the tools necessary to maximize their students' learning potential.

"While teachers are the initial beneficiaries of our programs," says Mr. Canter, "students are our true focal point; and it is to this group that our company is dedicated."

Lee Canter's views on education have been aired on the "Today" and "Oprah" television shows, among others. Articles about his work have been featured in *Newsweek* and many state and local publications.

Lee Canter & Associates has published more than 40 books and 10 professional-development video programs designed to help educators and parents raise happy, responsible, well-adjusted children.

Katia Petersen has more than 15 years of experience in child psychology, educational consulting, and teacher training. She has worked as the Violence Prevention Coordinator/Child Abuse Specialist in the St. Paul, Minnesota, public schools for six years and has authored a number of curriculum texts on conflict resolution and violence prevention. As the lead consultant for Argo & Associates, Ms. Petersen trains teachers around the country in conflict-resolution and violence-prevention strategies. She also mentors teachers in the classroom on techniques for helping students get along.

Says Ms. Petersen of her collaboration with Lee Canter: "In working with Lee, I discovered firsthand that he is a model of prosocial behavior: He listens, he shares, he treats others and their ideas with respect. With his wisdom and guidance, you'll find that you can help your students learn and demonstrate these same skills."

How to Use this Book

Teaching Students To Get Along provides you with the theoretical foundations for teaching and reinforcing prosocial skills and with practical lessons to help you create a more caring, cooperative classroom environment.

Chapter Topics

In each of the eight chapters, you will learn the rationale for the issues discussed. In addition to theories and concepts offered, useful guidelines and practical strategies are presented for transforming your classroom into a well-managed community. When these strategies are implemented and the lessons are taught, students have an optimal chance of internalizing and displaying the behaviors that will improve their chances for success in school.

Lesson Plans

I have the right to be treated with respect.

There are 21 lessons in *Teaching Students To Get Along.* For many of the theoretical foundations presented in each chapter, you will find a ready-to-teach lesson. The lessons—identified by a sketch of a "student," such as the one pictured—include the following elements:

■ Primary Outcome

A measurable objective that will help you determine the lesson's success.

■ Anticipatory Set

An opening activity or discussion designed to attract students' attention and introduce the lesson skill or strategy.

■ Instruction

A step-by-step process in which the topic is defined, then presented, typically, with an antisocial response to a situation and a prosocial response. The instruction enlists students' participation in becoming aware of prosocial behavior and in learning what the skills are for demonstrating that behavior.

■ Application

An activity that involves students in demonstrating the skill or strategy.

■ Closure

An activity or discussion that helps students summarize what they have learned and offers a means of gauging their understanding.

■ Follow-up Activity

Designed to be done the same day or as soon after the initial lesson as possible, this activity reviews, reinforces and extends what students have learned. Many activities involve creating a product that can go into students' portfolios.

■ Home Study Activity

An activity set at home that has students apply the skills learned. Some activities get families involved in helping to reinforce students' development of prosocial skills and strategies.

■ Student Worksheets

Reproducible student worksheets used in many of the lessons support the application and the activities.

Customizing the Lessons for Your Students and Your Teaching Style

Most lessons distinguish how to use the activities for teaching younger and older elementary students. In some cases, the lessons are geared to older students only; however, you may decide that a lesson is suitable to your younger students, in which case you can adapt the instruction as necessary.

You may prefer to use these lessons as blueprints for developing your own lesson plans. Keep in mind the following points as you teach skills and concepts for helping students get along:

- Use age-appropriate activities, to help children fully understand the concepts and grasp them faster.

- Be creative! Put the same effort and ingenuity into teaching these skills as you do into presenting academic skills. For example, primary-age children respond well to puppet skits and storytelling activities. Older students respond to more sophisticated techniques, such as role playing, imaging, and small-group discussions.

- Involve students in the lesson. Seek their questions, reactions, and responses.

- Summarize the key messages or have students summarize for you.

To make the lessons more relevant to students, look for opportunities to weave the issues in this book into subjects you are already teaching. All the lessons may be easily integrated into curriculum. The ability for people to get along with one another is a topic that is pertinent to most subject matter you teach. For example, take advantage of the current events you discuss in social studies to raise prosocial issues. Science studies referring to the environment may suggest addressing conflicts between groups of people with varied interests. Both language arts and history can be a starting point for teaching students about how to resolve problems when there are characters or personalities in conflict.

Whether teaching the lessons in this book or those of your own, remember that students won't master these skills and strategies the first time they're presented. Repeat the lessons and build into your day plenty of opportunities for students to practice listening, taking turns, negotiating, and so on. You'll find ideas and suggestions throughout the text for integrating getting-along skills into your curriculum and classroom routines.

How It Works for Me

In each chapter are first-person interviews with teachers who have successfully learned, then implemented in their classrooms HOW IT... the techniques and strategies presented in this book. In every case, these teachers were eager to share how teaching their students prosocial skills has benefited the learning experience.

Great Ideas

Several of the chapters offer added activities and information for how you can expand on the concepts taught. These "great ideas" contribute to the depth of your instruction.

CHAPTER 1

Creating a Caring Classroom Community

Fights on the playground… teasing in the lunchroom… bullying on the schoolbus… put-downs in the classroom… Does it seem to you that you spend more time than ever resolving disputes and soothing hurt feelings when you should be—and want to be— teaching?

Among a teacher's many hats, "peace officer" has always been one. You've always been expected to stop skirmishes between students and get to the bottom of each conflict. But time was when teachers could also expect most children to know—with a reminder now and then—how to take turns, share, ask politely, say "please" and "thank you," and treat peers with respect; time was when most children knew how to keep strong emotions in check. Today that's frequently not the case with more and more students. From kindergarten-age on up, far too many children come to school not only without the necessary social skills to get along with others, but with an inability to cope with frustration and control anger.

Like many teachers, you may feel frustrated by the lack of civility in your classroom. Your training as a teacher focused on helping children learn academic skills and knowledge. Most teachers don't have a ready reservoir of tried-and-tested lessons for teaching students the basic social skills that enable them to get along.

And, in truth, you may feel that you shouldn't have to teach these skills. It's understandable to resent losing valuable teaching time settling

fights and working through student differences when it happens day in and day out; to resent having to take on a larger chunk of a role that rightfully belongs to a child's parents and extended family.

But fair or not, to have a caring classroom community, *you* have to create that environment. You have to teach students prosocial skills. And with the help of the strategies and lessons in this resource book, you can. This chapter will help you see the advantages of teaching students to get along.

When Kids Fear Kids…

We know that the first step in solving a problem is defining it. What do we mean by students who don't know how to get along? They are children who believe that it's okay to be verbally abusive—to taunt and tease peers—and to be physically abusive—to push, shove, kick, hit. They are students who frequently engage in negative behavior on a scale that is unprecedented. Statistics like the following demonstrate the extent of the problem:

- Every year, over three million children in America report being intimidated, threatened with physical violence, or actually physically assaulted in school.

- Fifty percent of all boys in America state they were in a fight within the last year.

- Twenty-eight percent of all girls state they were in a fight within the last year.
- Every day, 160,000 children across America do not come to school because they are afraid someone will bully or harass them.

Sure, there have always been fights in school. There have always been children who teased or taunted others. What's different now is the magnitude of the aggressive behavior—the large numbers of students who are angry and abusive; the numbers of students who are constantly fearful in school.

The Roots of Antisocial Behavior

Why so much antisocial behavior today? One problem can be traced to parenting practices. A greater number of parents today are too permissive or absent in their children's lives, so that they don't teach their children manners, "the Golden Rule," and other prosocial skills. In homes where children are indulged and discipline is ineffective, they often don't learn how to cooperate, take turns, share, or say "I'm sorry." Nor do children learn why such actions are necessary in order to get along with others.

The other profound problem that affects many children's behavior in big and small ways is the overall increase in violence in our society. Violence saturates the cartoons, TV shows, video games, and movies that children view; violent themes—often inspired by television and movies—pervade children's own imaginative play. Few children are immune to such "entertainment" violence. For a smaller number of children at much greater risk, violence is a fact of life in the neighborhoods where they live. And most troubling of all, scores of children see violence in their own homes. For many students, intimidation and

lashing out verbally and physically are the only approaches to problem solving they know.

While the debate continues in many circles about the degree to which violence on television and in the movies *really* impacts children's behavior, teachers know that children often imitate the karate chops, kicks, and other violent actions of their TV "heroes." It is often the antisocial behavior that children see around them that breeds the antisocial behavior you see at school.

Taunting, Teasing, Bullying, and More

What kinds of problems with students getting along do teachers most often have in their classrooms? You may recognize some of these: Teachers report problems with elementary students, both boys and girls, getting into fights because of name calling. They report students as young as first grade forming cliques and isolating children they don't accept into their groups. The playground in particular is the site of many problems with students fighting, taunting, and bullying one another. Teachers are even reporting cases of sexual harassment among students.

The changing demographics of our schools also creates tensions among students. More and more schools are a mix of cultures. Students speak languages their peers don't understand and have customs, traditions, and allegiances that are foreign to others. All too easily, prejudice, ignorance, or innocent misunderstandings can lead to fights between students.

How Fear Affects Learning

As a result of the problems students bring with them to the classroom, teachers end up being referee, judge, and cop. For the nonaggressive students, trying to learn alongside abusive peers spawns fear and anxiety. Research has demonstrated the link between students' perceived sense of safety and their ability to learn. [Edmonds, 1982] Students must feel the school grounds and common areas are safe, but also that they will not be victimized by other students. Students must feel that their teachers will intervene to protect them if they are victimized by others. When children don't feel safe—when they are preoccupied with what's going to happen in the lunchroom, on the playground, or during the walk or bus ride home—their ability to learn is diminished. And as the statistics show, far too many students don't even have the chance to learn, because they're too afraid to come to school at all.

But the students who are on the receiving end of bullying behavior aren't the only ones who lose out. Students who lack the social skills to interact appropriately with their peers often lash out because they feel alienated and rejected. Studies show that students who lack a connection to peers and teachers, who never feel at home in school, are at risk of dropping out. And unchecked, aggressive behavior in elementary school can escalate as students get older. The children who bully on the playground today may be tomorrow's adolescent criminals.

Changing the Climate in Your Classroom Community

The first step in turning around students' antisocial behavior is recognizing that while you may not be able to reduce the level of aggression in society at large, you can make a difference in your own classroom. Prosocial behaviors are skills that children can learn, just as they learn

the academic skills to read, write, and compute. Many children have simply not been taught how to cooperate, share, try to understand another person's point of view, be tolerant, and treat others as they would want to be treated. With organization and a plan, you can teach children how to interact with peers and work through differences in nonviolent ways.

Start by thinking about your classroom as a community. By virtue of your position as teacher and adult, you are the leader of that community. Your students are citizens of it. Just as a real community sets rules and guidelines for behavior that ensure the peace and safety of its citizens, you need to do the same in your classroom. And just as most citizens follow the rules set by their communities, once your young citizens know and understand your expectations for prosocial behavior, most will try to meet those expectations. Children want to feel safe in your classroom, and they will welcome behavior boundaries that help ensure their safety.

Research also confirms what many teachers know from experience about what helps students feel safe in the classroom. A sense of order marked by explicitly stated and reinforced rules and procedures helps to create a safe and comfortable learning environment.

The Value of Teaching Students to Get Along

Why make teaching prosocial skills a priority in your classroom when there are so many other demands on your time and curriculum? Estimate the amount of time you spend each day responding to problems between students. It might be a little bit or it might be a lot, but whatever it is, it's lost instructional time.

On the other hand, teaching prosocial skills is a constructive activity. It promotes a calmer classroom environment. It creates a setting where consideration of others and trust is the norm. And it enables you to focus on teaching and students to focus on learning.

These aren't strategies that work for only some teachers in some schools. In preparing the graduate course on which this book is based, we had the opportunity to work in classrooms across the country, in all socioeconomic areas. And we've seen teachers learn and utilize simple strategies that have enabled them to set up safe, caring classrooms. Research confirms our observations: Teachers who take the time to teach prosocial expectations have much more cooperative, conflict-free classrooms.

But promoting a more positive classroom environment is actually a short-term benefit of teaching students to get along. There are also these important long-term benefits for all students:

- **You promote tolerance and understanding by celebrating diversity.** When you help children—particularly those of different cultures—understand one another, you help them see the similarities that unite all peoples. Once students recognize that they are all more alike than different, they're better able to learn from and enjoy the qualities that make cultures—and individuals—unique. Developing this understanding in the elementary years can shape children's views of themselves and others all through life. We make giant steps toward creating a more harmonious world when we help students learn to appreciate diversity. ★*Lesson #1: Appreciating Diversity*, on page 13, helps students recognize and appreciate the similarities and differences among class members. Also, on page 17, you will find suggestions for additional activities that promote understanding among students.

- **You foster children's resiliency.** We talk a lot about "at-risk" students in education today, and for good reason. There are more and more children who are adversely affected by poverty, neglect, abuse, divorce and single parenthood, and violence on the streets and in their homes. Yet, a growing body of research also points to the strong influence teachers can have in helping students overcome these problems and develop into healthy, responsible, competent adults. And the factors that help build resiliency are also those that contribute to developing prosocial skills. For example, a caring classroom environment greatly benefits at-risk students, as does holding positive expectations for students' behavior and academic performance. Giving students jobs in the classroom and in the school at large helps them shoulder responsibility and feel a part of the learning community.

- **You teach students valuable job skills.** Interpersonal skills are key to a worker's success. We know that intuitively, but the 1992 SCANS Report stated it conclusively. SCANS (Secretary of Labor's Commission on Necessary Skills) identifies five main competencies that every worker needs and that schools beginning in the elementary years should instill in students:

  - Resources (identifies, organizes, and allocates resources);

  - Information (acquires and uses information);

  - Systems (understands complex interrelationships);

  - Technology (works with a variety of technologies);

  - **Interpersonal (works with others).** Among the interpersonal skills identified by the SCANS authors as important are learning to cooperate and work as a team— skills that we recognize as essential for our classrooms to function well.

- **You offer students life skills.** The student who can't get along with peers today is at risk of being the adult who can't get along on the job, the relative or spouse who can't get along with the rest of the family, the neighbor who can't get along with the people next door, the citizen who can't get along in society. When you help students learn how to negotiate their differences, respect the rights of others, and see themselves as vital members of a group, you provide students with the tools of social success that will help them build a productive life. The ability to get along with others isn't just a school skill; it's a life skill.

their peers. There will be disagreements. It's how they respond to conflict that matters.

Your primary goal is to teach students how to respond in *nonviolent* ways. Show children how to solve problems with words of understanding and compromise, how to find solutions that make both parties feel like winners. So many students lack these skills. They return name calling with name calling; they answer force with force. Somebody gives them a "hard look," so they give a hard look back, escalating the confrontation. By giving students alternatives to aggression in resolving differences, you give them a vital life skill that may save their life someday.

Conflict—It's Natural

Teaching students prosocial skills doesn't mean that you'll eliminate all conflict from your classroom. That's an impossible goal, because conflict is a natural, common state. There will always be disagreements among students. There will always be situations where students want the same thing. Emotions like anger and frustration—normal, human emotions—will trigger confrontations between students.

And conflict is not always a bad thing. Conflict can be a catalyst for problem solving. Conflict can force students to see another point of view—and learn from the experience. Negotiating our differences and learning to see strength in diversity is essentially what makes life interesting and vibrant. Try to imagine a classroom where there is no conflict, where everyone thinks alike and always agrees. Is that really a classroom where you would be challenged as a teacher, where you'd enjoy teaching?

Part of your task in helping students learn to get along is to help them recognize that conflict is natural. They won't always see eye to eye with

Turning Around Behavior Takes Time

Children can be taught prosocial skills, but they don't learn them in a day. Like learning to read, learning to get along with others takes practice and patience. It requires working at these skills constantly. It involves building them into your curriculum, so that you're reinforcing these skills in a dozen ways all through the school day. It demands that you and all of the adults with whom students interact be models of prosocial behavior. It means making a commitment and making the time to create a caring community in your classroom.

You'll find plenty of help with teaching prosocial skills and behaviors throughout this book. You'll find guidance in developing preventive strategies for avoiding conflict and violence and in helping children learn how to stand up to bullying behavior. Specifically, you'll find information and activities related to the following topics:

- Establishing prosocial expectations that encourage students to get along.

- Teaching specific prosocial skills—such as attentive and active listening, paying compliments, understanding others' feelings—and helping students practice these essential life skills on a daily basis.

- Structuring a daily forum for discussing issues related to how children are getting along; for promoting positive interactions among students; and for helping students get to know others better.

- Building on the power of cooperative-learning groups to foster students' ability to work as part of a team.

- Teaching students strategies for dealing effectively with everyday conflicts: how to stand up for themselves, how to stop and think before they act when they are angry, how to resolve conflicts so that everyone wins.

- Identifying the causes of bullying behavior and teaching students strategies to respond effectively to such behavior.

- Working with colleagues to create a schoolwide campaign that supports your efforts at promoting a safe, caring environment in your classroom.

On the next page, "How It Works for Me" describes one teacher's success with implementing several of these strategies in her classroom. In subsequent chapters, you will read of other colleagues' experiences with teaching their students prosocial skills.

Assessing Where to Begin

To determine your own awareness of prosocial expectations and teaching techniques, make a copy of the Teacher Assessment on page 9, then answer it. Don't worry if you find yourself checking "sometimes" or "seldom" a lot. This book is designed to help you increase your understanding of the importance of teaching prosocial skills and to offer you lessons for doing so. Retake the survey in a few months, to gauge your own growth in this area.

Use the Student Survey on page 11 to get a sense of how students think their classmates get along, as well as whether they feel safe in and around the school building and grounds. With younger children, you'll want to adapt the questions to their understanding and discuss them as a group. Invite older students to fill out the questionnaire on their own. Let students answer anonymously, to encourage greater honesty. The survey can provide valuable information that will help you determine what kinds of problems students have in getting along and how best to help. Repeat the survey in a few months or midyear, as a means of checking your progress in teaching prosocial skills.

And be sure to let parents know of your efforts to establish a caring classroom community for their children by sending home the letter on page 16.

Looking Ahead to a More Peaceful Classroom

You know that it's not enjoyable to teach or to learn in a classroom where students are "at each other" all the time. It creates a feeling that students don't care about one another, that they don't care about learning, that they don't care about you. The hopelessness and sense of powerlessness such feelings can produce can easily lead to burnout.

Protect your students and protect yourself by teaching the skills and strategies that enable children to get along with others. The lessons in this book may be some of the most important you ever teach.

Help Students Get Ready for Their Futures by Celebrating Diversity

Our school is a diverse mix of students, with kids from different cultures and socioeconomic levels. In one class, for example, I'll have fifth-graders who come to school without socks or who wear the same shirt all week and those who come from affluent homes and have all the clothes and electronic toys they could want.

Invariably, there are kids who don't get along. They label each other; they pick on each other.

I believe that it's our job as teachers to prepare students for their futures in the workforce. Students have to know how to work with others, how to cooperate, how to share tasks to get an assignment done. Most students aren't going to have jobs where they're sitting alone at their desk, doing their own thing. They're going to be interacting with others.

To give my students more opportunities to learn to work with others, I've started doing more instruction in cooperative groups. But for the groups to be effective, I've had to tackle the issue of diversity. We spend a lot of time at the beginning of the year talking about our differences and how they are a source of strength. We discuss what we can learn about each other's cultures and customs. We also recognize our different talents. For example, one student in a group may not be a good reader, but he or she may be a skilled artist who can illustrate stories or draw diagrams for the team.

I also work to demonstrate through my own behavior that I celebrate the diversity in my classroom. We have to be honest: Teachers do label students. We can succumb to stereotypes, and we have to fight against that. I consciously try to model through my behavior that I believe every student is capable, that every student has something worthwhile to contribute to the group.

My students do get along better. I really see the rewards of celebrating diversity when my students come together with others in our fifth-grade team. My students don't tend to congregate by racial groups; boys aren't afraid to sit by girls. It's not easy to overcome cultural or economic differences; it takes time to change students' behavior and our own. But I feel that by helping my students learn to cooperate with all of their peers, I'm truly helping them get ready to be more successful workers in the future.

Pat Mueller, Glenview Middle School
East Moline, Illinois

Teaching My Students to Get Along

Before writing on the assessment form, make copies for future self-evaluation. Be sure to use this assessment tool periodically during the school year.

Complete the assessment to determine areas in which you are now utilizing effective skills and those in which you need to improve. As you proceed through this book, be aware of the areas in which you need to improve and concentrate on learning new information and skills.

Read each statement and check the appropriate response.

	Consistently	Sometimes	Seldom
1. I establish clear prosocial expectations in my classroom.	☐	☐	☐
2. I develop age-appropriate lessons to teach my students prosocial expectations.	☐	☐	☐
3. I plan activities to increase students' ability to recognize the behavior choices they have, and to choose prosocial behaviors.	☐	☐	☐
4. I am consistent in enforcing classroom expectations.	☐	☐	☐
5. I develop a sense of community within my classroom.	☐	☐	☐
6. I use modeling techniques and teachable moments to reinforce prosocial expectations.	☐	☐	☐
7. I reinforce prosocial expectations by integrating lessons into my academic curriculum.	☐	☐	☐
8. I conduct a daily class meeting to discuss issues regarding prosocial skills and expectations.	☐	☐	☐
9. I use cooperative-learning structures in my classroom.	☐	☐	☐
10. I use effective strategies to communicate expectations and monitor students when they work in cooperative groups.	☐	☐	☐
11. I use techniques that require students to be accountable for their performance in cooperative-group activities.	☐	☐	☐

Continued

	Consistently	Sometimes	Seldom
12. I design cooperative-group activities that promote interdependence and build group cohesiveness.	☐	☐	☐
13. I teach students prosocial behaviors such as being a good listener, giving compliments, showing empathy, and treating each other with respect.	☐	☐	☐
14. I teach students the difference between, and the potential outcomes of, effective and ineffective responses to conflict.	☐	☐	☐
15. I teach students skills for responding to conflict situations in an assertive (not passive or hostile) manner.	☐	☐	☐
16. I teach students how to recognize their anger and manage angry feelings in a peaceful, prosocial manner.	☐	☐	☐
17. I view conflict as a normal part of life and utilize student conflicts as opportunities to teach essential life skills.	☐	☐	☐
18. I teach students conflict resolution skills and provide many opportunities to practice these skills.	☐	☐	☐
19. I teach my students negotiating skills to encourage them to help one another resolve conflicts between their peers.	☐	☐	☐
20. I maintain a no-tolerance stance to bullying behavior (I do not view bullying as simply a passing phase of childhood).	☐	☐	☐
21. I institute classwide rules that address bullying behavior.	☐	☐	☐
22. I teach victims of bullies specific skills that enable them to stand up for themselves.	☐	☐	☐
23. I consistently enforce schoolwide prosocial expectations.	☐	☐	☐
24. I work as a team with my colleagues and administrator to promote and encourage prosocial skills throughout the school community.	☐	☐	☐
25. I continually assess the effectiveness of my efforts and plan accordingly for improvement.	☐	☐	☐

STUDENT SURVEY
Getting Along in School

In order for you to do your best work in school, you need to feel safe and you need to get along with other students. Tell me how you feel. Please answer each question honestly. You don't have to put your name on the paper.

1. I think most students in this class get along with each other. ☐ Yes ☐ No

   If no, why do you think so? _____

   _____

2. I think most students in this school get along with each other. ☐ Yes ☐ No

   If no, why do you think so? _____

   _____

3. I have been teased by students in my class. ☐ Yes ☐ No

   If yes, where? _____

   How often (such as once in a while, every week, every day)?

   _____

4. I have been teased by students in other classes. ☐ Yes ☐ No

   If yes, where? _____

   How often (such as once in a while, every week, every day)?

   _____

5. I have been in verbal fights (shouting, name calling) with students in my class.
   ☐ Yes ☐ No

   If yes, where? _____

   How often (such as once in a while, every week, every day)?

   _____

6. I have been in verbal fights (shouting, name calling) with students in other classes.
   ☐ Yes ☐ No

   If yes, where? _____

   How often (such as once in a while, every week, every day)?

   _____

7. I have been in physical fights (kicking, hitting) with students in my class.
   ☐ Yes ☐ No

Continued

If yes, where? _____

How often (such as once in a while, every week, every day)?

_____

8. I have been in physical fights (kicking, hitting) with students in other classes.
☐ Yes ☐ No

If yes, where? _____

How often (such as once in a while, every week, every day)?

_____

9. Have you seen verbal or physical fights between students in these places?

Working in small groups in the classroom ☐ Yes ☐ No

If yes, how often (rarely, frequently, every day)? _____

In the bathroom ☐ Yes ☐ No

If yes, how often (rarely, frequently, every day)? _____

In the cafeteria ☐ Yes ☐ No

If yes, how often (rarely, frequently, every day)? _____

On the playground ☐ Yes ☐ No

If yes, how often (rarely, frequently, every day)? _____

On the schoolbus ☐ Yes ☐ No

If yes, how often (rarely, frequently, every day)? _____

10. Have you ever been afraid in any of these places?

In your classroom ☐ Yes ☐ No   If yes, please tell why: _____

_____

In the bathroom ☐ Yes ☐ No   If yes, please tell why: _____

_____

In the cafeteria ☐ Yes ☐ No   If yes, please tell why: _____

_____

On the playground ☐ Yes ☐ No If yes, please tell why: _____

_____

On the schoolbus ☐ Yes ☐ No If yes, please tell why: _____

_____

Lesson #1

APPRECIATING DIVERSITY

Everybody is different in some way.

PRIMARY OUTCOME

Students will be able to recognize differences between themselves and others and demonstrate the need for accepting diversity in order to get along with each other in the classroom.

MATERIALS NEEDED

Closure: "Kids Are Different" reproducible, page 15

ANTICIPATORY SET

Read the poem, "Kids Are Different." Ask students how kids in the poem were different from one another. Say, "Sometimes when people are different, and have different ideas, they don't understand each other, or they're scared of each other, or they don't like each other. When this happens, they have a problem getting along together. You are going to learn how important it is to understand and accept the differences in other people so it can help us get along better in this classroom."

INSTRUCTION

1. Guide students in a discussion about human differences (gender, race, country, language, customs, age, physical, intelligence, appearance). Have students add to the list. List the terms on the board and define them.

Ask students if they think it is all right to be different or if it would be better if we were all exactly the same.

2. Ask students what kinds of differences between people they have observed. Ask how the differences made them feel, adding that it is okay to have feelings about it. Then ask what kind of differences they observe between people in the classroom. "There are a lot of differences between people in this classroom. We are not all exactly the same; we are all different in some way."

3. "Sometimes the differences cause problems. Have you ever seen a situation where a classmate or someone else was put down, laughed at or ignored because the person was different in some way? Do we want people in our classroom to be treated like that?"

4. "How can differences make our lives better?" Guide students in a discussion (differences can bring us new friends, new customs, new ideas, and new ways of living and working together) and list the results on the board. "How would it feel to bring these new things into this classroom and into your lives?"

5. "To bring the benefits of being different into our lives, we need to accept and appreciate the differences between people. When differences between people cause problems, we are going to be learning over the next few weeks what to do about it, so that everybody in this classroom can get along better."

APPLICATION

Ask students to form groups and tell them to brainstorm answers to the following questions: 1) In this group, how are we the same? (same school, class, group, height, hair color) 2) In this group, how are we different? (boys, girls, religion, family, height, hair color). Ask younger students to respond aloud; older students can respond from a list the group has made. Then ask how they can use their differences to help them work and get along better together.

CLOSURE

"Your answers showed that people in this classroom are alike in some ways and are different in some ways. We are going to admire and celebrate the differences because it means that you will all be contributing something unique to our class. It is the differences among us that will bring us new information, give us energy, and make us think. When we celebrate and accept our differences, there will be fewer problems and we will all get along better with each other." Give each student a copy of the "Kids Are Different" poem to keep. ∎

Follow-Up Activity

Have students in small groups cut out pictures from magazines or catalogs showing all kinds of people: young, old, various ethnic groups, etc. Ask each group to assemble a collage, then post the completed work on the wall. Ask each group to explain what is unique about each person in their picture. Conduct a discussion on what the word "American" means.

For more follow-up ideas for this lesson, see "Great Ideas: Activities Promoting Awareness of Diversity," page 17.

Home Study Activity

In class, have primary students draw a picture depicting people from various cultures and with different abilities. Ask students to take their drawing home and tell a story to their families about what the people have in common. Intermediate students may create a list instead of a drawing. Examples of commonalities:

- All people have the same basic needs for shelter, food, air, love, etc.

- All people have bodies with skin, blood, a heart, etc.

- All people have feelings.

Kids Are Different

Kids are diff'rent
We don't even look the same
Some kids speak diff'rent languages
We all have a different name
Kids are different
But if you look inside you'll see
That tall kid, that small kid
Is just like you and me,
Some folks are surprised that
Kids in wheelchairs play
Blind kids read, deaf kids talk
Except in a diff'rent way.
Able kids, disabled kids
There's nothing we can't do
Just take a look inside yourself
You'll be so proud of you
Because
Kids are diff'rent
We don't even look the same
Some kids speak diff'rent languages
We all have a different name.
Kids are diff'rent
But if you look inside you'll see
That tall kid, that small kid
That deaf kid, that blind kid
Are just like you and me.

From "Kids on the Block." Lyrics, Barbara Aiello; Music, Bud Forrest.
Permission to reprint granted to all who wish to reproduce the words to this song.

Dear Parent,

This year I will be teaching your child more than math, social studies and language arts.

As a teacher committed to establishing a peaceful and caring classroom, I will also be teaching your child more about how to get along with others—what it takes in the way of cooperation and respect, and what it returns in the way of dignity and self-esteem.

This year, students will be learning such skills as being good listeners, treating each other with respect, sharing, displaying empathy, learning to "stop, think and act" in the face of conflict, and standing up to bullying behavior.

In addition, my students and I will meet daily to talk and share feelings about their problems, conflicts, successes and achievements in the classroom.

Your family is an important resource in promoting our caring classroom and ensuring the success of your children. Your involvement in the social-skills activities your child will do at home sends a message that knowing how to get along with others is important.

Working together, we can create a climate of equality and pride for our students that promotes a safe and caring environment.

Sincerely,

Activities Promoting Awareness of Diversity

Holding Hands

Have each student cut out a tracing of his or her hand. Ask them to write the following: on the thumb, their name; on the second and third fingers, two reasons why they think they are the same as others in the class; on the fourth and little finger, two reasons why they think they are different. Have students draw a picture of themselves in the palm and then cut out their artwork. Post the hands around the classroom in one chain, with every two hands facing each other with the middle fingers touching.

Promises to Keep

Tell students that you are going to list on the board some activities for appreciating the differences in each other. They are to select one of the ideas and write it down ("I promise to. . .") together with their name and the date you set for completing the activities. Some ideas for these "mini" contracts are:

- I will be partner for a day with a new student and help to make him or her feel comfortable in our classroom.

- I will try to get to know a person with whom I have been unfriendly.

- I will eat lunch with someone I have had an argument with.

- I will choose someone who I feel is different from me and try to get to know him or her better.

- I will choose someone whose family celebrates different holidays than mine and find out more about their customs.

- I will choose a student who was born in another country, or whose close family member was, and find out more about the person's background.

When the activities have been performed, call on volunteers to describe and evaluate their experiences (or have students write a paper).

Bread Brings Us Together

Tell students that most cultures consume bread in some form because it is nutritious and relatively easy to make. Emphasize how different groups of people use the essentially simple ingredients for bread in various and creative ways, according to their cultures (wheat bread, French bread, tortillas, pita, nann, flat breads, lavash, rye). Here are some ideas for connecting the similarities and differences in bread-making to diversity among people:

- Conduct a class survey to see what different kinds of bread are eaten at home, and ask for volunteers to bring samples to class.

- Have the class research and study the history of of breads made in various parts of the United States and in other countries.

- Have a bread-baking—and bread-eating—day, using students' family recipes.

- Visit a bakery after students have studied bread in diverse cultures (they will be more apt to appreciate the experience).

Skin Test

Tell students to arrange themselves in a circle. Ask them to look around the circle and compare the color of the skin on their hands. Some differences in color will be obvious right away. Have students look closely at the skin tones that appear to be similar and see if they can detect the more subtle differences (yellow, pink or olive tones). Ask students to try to find a crayon color (or create a paint color) that is closest to their hand color, and have them make a paper mural showing everybody's hand and its skin tone.

Our Family Tree

Create a bulletin board with a tall paper tree with a branch for each student in the room. Give students one "leaf" for each member of their family. Students write each name (including aunts, uncles, grandparents—anyone whom they consider family, even the dog) on a leaf and "attach" them to their branch. Over the course of a week, have students add photos, sentences about family customs and small drawings of family members to their branch. At the end of the week, have all students describe their families. Conduct a discussion about the similarities (all students are in a family) and differences (all families will be different).

CHAPTER 2

Setting Prosocial Expectations

Like most teachers, you probably have rules that define how you want students to behave so that they can learn in your classroom. You wouldn't just assume students know these behaviors—in a well-run classroom, you wouldn't leave that to chance.

Why, then, do we often expect children to just know how to get along with others? Some of the assumptions we make undoubtedly stem from how we grew up. We were taught by parents, grandparents, probably neighbors, too, to treat people as we would want to be treated, to respect others' property. But there is all-too-ample proof that many of our students are learning far different lessons at home and on the streets about how people treat one another. If we don't state clearly how we expect students to behave, they'll resort to the "communication" techniques they know: verbal and physical threats and actions.

Setting prosocial expectations—and teaching students how to behave in the ways you expect them to—is the first step in teaching students to get along. This chapter will set you on the right course toward achieving a caring classroom community.

Establishing Prosocial Rules

Setting expectations for prosocial behavior will help you and your students feel more comfortable in your classroom. Remember that as the leader of your classroom community, students look to you for guidance. Children want to feel safe in your classroom. They want to know that you will take care of them. They want to know the boundaries of acceptable behavior.

How are prosocial expectations different from your classroom rules? Prosocial expectations focus specifically on how children interact with one another. They need to apply on the playground as well as in the lunchroom, in the classroom as well as on the schoolbus. Your classroom rules are designed to ensure a smooth-running *classroom*. While some rules may pertain to student interactions, others, such as "Stay in your seat unless you have permission to move about the room" relate to general classroom management. By having a separate set of expectations for how children will get along, you demonstrate to students that how they treat one another—even when they are not in your presence—is very important to you.

Involve students in developing prosocial expectations for the class. In this chapter, ★*Lesson #2: Creating Prosocial Expectations*, on page 23, teaches children why prosocial rules are needed and involves them in setting expectations. Here are three guidelines that will help increase the success of your rules.

- **Fewer rules are better.** You can't regulate every interaction students have, so don't overwhelm them with too many rules. Limit your list to no more than five. Think about the behaviors that will have the biggest impact in helping students get along. Then put those in the form of positive expectations.

- **Set very specific rules.** Any rule that is open to interpretation will not be effective. Avoid such rules as "Be nice": Older elementary students may have a very different definition of "nice" behavior from your own. The best rules are those that state what behavior is expected, such as "Keep hands and feet to yourself." You can easily tell by observing or listening to children whether a rule has been broken.

- **Set rules that are developmentally appropriate for your age group.** On their own, preschoolers and kindergartners may not know what "cooperate" means, but they do understand what it means to "work together and help each other." Use words that your students will understand, and match the concepts you're teaching with what your children can grasp.

When setting rules, remember that the expectations must fit your classroom and your students. Here are five possible prosocial expectations. Adapt them to fit your particular needs.

- Listen when others are speaking.

- No put-downs.

- No teasing.

- Keep hands and feet to yourself.

- Treat others the way you would want to be treated.

An overriding theme for everything that pertains to prosocial expectations is what is commonly known as "the golden rule": Treat others the way you would want to be treated. Although this "rule" may seem open to interpretation and not specific, the concept is an ideal that is attainable through the practice of the prosocial skills taught in this book. Therefore, a high standard of behavior such as this is a recommended expectation for your classroom.

Teaching Prosocial Rules

Setting rules isn't enough to ensure students will follow them. You have to be sure children understand the rules by showing them the behavior you expect when they follow each of the rules. Therefore, you must teach your prosocial rules to students.

In this chapter you'll find ★*Lesson #3: Treating Each Other with Respect*, page 27, and ★*Lesson #4: Dealing with "Put-Downs,"* page 31. (For two lessons on listening skills, see Chapter 3.) You'll also find a Classroom Pledge on page 29 that asks every student to promise to treat others with respect. Once every student has signed it, congratulate the class and post the pledge in a prominent place in the room.

You may want to develop your own lessons for teaching students why they must keep hands and feet to themselves, why teasing is hurtful, and for understanding other expectations that are important to you and your students. Remember to use age-appropriate activities in teaching these rules and to involve students by seeking their questions and responses.

Repeat each lesson at least once. Students aren't likely to internalize the prosocial rules the first time they hear them, anymore than they fully grasp any new concept you teach. You know the reality: It takes practice, practice, practice to learn new skills.

Setting Consequences for Inappropriate Behavior

You've identified your expectations and shown students what behaviors you want to see from them. Now there's one more critical step in setting prosocial expectations: You have to back up those expectations with actions. Students must know that consequences will occur if they treat a peer in an inappropriate way.

Choosing Consequences

Identify a set of consequences and post them on a chart. Make a verbal warning the consequence for any first offense. To demonstrate your fairness, you always want to give students a chance to amend their behavior.

From working with classroom teachers, we've found that the most effective consequences have a logical connection to the rule that's been broken. For example, you have the class in a circle on the floor for a group discussion. One student is elbowing another. The rule is "Keep hands and feet to yourself." The consequence of breaking that rule a second time is separation and removal from the group.

Or let's say a student is teasing another child or calling him or her names. The consequence for breaking the "No teasing" or "No put-downs" rule more than once is a verbal or written apology.

Here are a few more guidelines for setting consequences.

- **Make consequences unpleasant, but not unjust.** A consequence should never physically hurt or humiliate a student.

- **Make consequences age appropriate.** Draw on your knowledge of your age group when setting consequences, to be sure they'll be meaningful for your students.

- **Make consequences ones you can enforce easily.** You must be consistent in applying consequences. Therefore, be sure the consequences you choose are ones you are comfortable with and can enforce every time.

Presenting Consequences

When you teach your prosocial behaviors, introduce the consequences, too. Help students see that the rules and consequences are parts of a whole—your total commitment to creating a caring classroom community.

Display your chart of consequences and read them aloud. With younger students, use a puppet or stuffed animal to explain what each consequence means and when it will be applied. With older students, explain each consequence, then ask volunteers to summarize for the class what you have said.

You'll also want to inform parents and your principal of your prosocial rules and consequences. Be sure to explain the purpose of your prosocial efforts, to help garner their support.

Remember, the key to administering consequences is consistency. Students must know that you are serious about expecting them to get along.

Know Your Students as Individuals

I've taught for 23 years in grades two, three, four, and five. I recently took a Lee Canter & Associates graduate course, "Teaching Students to Get Along," and it validated a lot of the strategies I've used successfully over the years to create a more cooperative classroom.

One of my biggest behavior problems was a fifth-grade girl who was very bright but had real difficulties in getting along with other students. She was multilingual and would swear in French or Spanish at the other students. She wanted her way all the time and had trouble with such skills as sharing, taking turns, and working as part of a team.

What helped turn around her behavior? Setting clear expectations for appropriate behavior, for one. This girl needed to know the boundaries of acceptable behavior. And from my experience, if you set expectations for how students will treat one another, most students will meet them.

I also make a conscious effort to get to know students as individuals. I realized that this particular girl needed attention and guidance. She needed to learn that she could get attention and even praise by cooperating with others and following our prosocial expectations.

You have to understand where your students are coming from: Why do they act out? Why don't they cooperate? What's going on in their lives that might cause this behavior? You have to make time to get to know each student. Here are some ways I build in that time:

- I eat lunch in my classroom and invite students to visit with me.

- I make myself available to students after school.

- I plan special projects that allow me to work with small groups of students at a time. For example, one fifth-grade project involves selling popcorn at school and using the profits to buy T-shirts with the project logo. Groups of five to six students at a time take turns helping to pop and bag the popcorn. Everyone who helps gets a T-shirt.

Nonacademic projects are great ways to get to know students on a personal level. Cooperating with peers on a project also builds teamwork skills. Everyone benefits when we make opportunities to get to know our students well.

Thomas Hart, West Sand Lake Elementary
West Sand Lake, New York

Lesson #2

CREATING PROSOCIAL EXPECTATIONS

Our rules help us to get along better.

PRIMARY OUTCOME

Students will illustrate or list the prosocial rules needed for them to get along in the classroom.

MATERIALS NEEDED

Application: Posterboard, art materials

Follow-Up Activity: "Getting Along in Our Classroom: How Am I Doing?" reproducible, page 25

Home Study Activity: "Our Rules for Getting Along in Our Classroom" reproducible, page 26

ANTICIPATORY SET

"I would like you all to close your eyes and pretend you're coming with me to visit two different classrooms that I am going to tell you about. Our visit to these two classrooms will help us understand how important it is to be able to get along with each other while we're in school."

INSTRUCTION

1. "With your eyes still closed, imagine a classroom where you don't feel safe and secure."

   • "It's noisy in that classroom, and people are running around doing and saying anything they want to."

   • "Think about what else might be happening in a classroom that isn't safe. Think about what the people might be saying to each other. Imagine how the students in that room are feeling."

   • "Now open your eyes and let's talk about what you saw in your minds." Elicit responses: People are: angry, hitting, yelling, getting hurt, getting their feelings hurt, not paying attention to the teacher.

2. "Now close your eyes again and imagine a classroom in which everybody does feel safe and secure." Describe: People keep their hands to themselves, don't yell or run or bump into anybody, don't take anything without asking, don't make fun of anybody, speak nicely to one another, can concentrate and pay attention.

3. Ask students to open their eyes. Compare and contrast the unsafe and safe classrooms. Ask students how the safe classroom helps us in school. Ask students which kind of classroom they would prefer.

4. "Now that we've decided what kind of classroom we like, let's talk about what we can do to make sure we have this kind of classroom and how we will expect each of us to act towards one another."

- Explain that the class will develop some rules that say how we expect everyone in the classroom to cooperate (words, actions, attitudes) so that we can get along better with each other in a respectful and safe way.

5. Preplan a few expectations for getting along together. (Note: You may want to include the expectations addressed in Lessons #3 and #4 in this chapter: "Treat others the way you would want to be treated," and "No put-downs.") Elicit no more than five rules from students, and clarify them. Write the rules on the board, then have the students chorally read them. Then say, "These are the rules for getting along together the class chose. Do we agree on them?"

APPLICATION

Use posterboard to have students in small groups design posters as follows. Rotate hanging each group's poster in the classroom for all students to see.

Intermediate: Have students create posters in their small groups listing the rules for getting along together. Monitor the students to make sure they are following the rules while they work.

Primary: List each rule on a poster. Have each group illustrate one of the rules for a safe classroom. Place the completed drawings next to the corresponding rule on the poster.

CLOSURE

"Following our rules helped you to get along together while you were working on your poster. Which rules were you following when you were working?" Call on students to respond. Then say, "In the next few days, we are going to learn how to practice our rules so that we will all be successful in getting along with one another in this classroom." ■

Follow-Up Activity

For the first two weeks after the class has chosen their prosocial rules, have students record daily in their journals their success in meeting the rules. At the end of each week, give each student a copy of the "Getting Along in Our Classroom: How Am I Doing?" reproducible and have students evaluate their success that week. Then discuss the results. Ask if there is one rule that is harder to follow than others, and if there is a rule they think should be added. (With primary students, conduct a daily discussion.)

Home Study Activity

Give each student a copy of the "Our Rules for Getting Along in Our Classroom" reproducible. Have older students list the rules and write a description of what the rules mean. (Younger students can draw pictures of a safe classroom.) Tell them to explain the rules to their parents. Ask students to choose one of the rules—such as, "Treat others the way you want to be treated"— to follow at home and report to the class on how it helped them get along with family or friends.

Name _____

GETTING ALONG IN OUR CLASSROOM
How Am I Doing?

For each classroom rule, write down if you are or are not having success in following it. If you are not, tell why not.

_____

_____

_____

_____

_____

_____

_____

_____

_____

_____

_____

_____

_____

_____

_____

_____

_____

_____

_____

_____

_____

Our Rules for Getting Along
in Our Classroom

TREATING EACH OTHER WITH RESPECT

I have the right to be treated with respect.

This lesson and Lesson #4, "Dealing with 'Put-Downs,'" teach behavior for two prosocial expectations that are suggested for your classroom.

PRIMARY OUTCOME

Students will identify how they would like to be treated and will be able to demonstrate being respectful to one another as it applies to interaction in the classroom.

MATERIALS NEEDED

Anticipatory Set: Primary—puppet or stuffed animal

Follow-Up Activity: "Classroom Pledge" reproducible, page 29

ANTICIPATORY SET

Primary: Use a puppet or stuffed animal to demonstrate disrespect by having the puppet say to the teacher: "Get out of my way! I want to be first in line!" Ask students if they would like to be treated this way. "Did the puppet care about me? Was the puppet respectful to me?" Tell students that they are going to learn more about what respect means and how it will help us get along with each other.

Intermediate: Walk to the back of the room and grab a student's book. Ask students if they thought you cared about the student and behaved respectfully. Tell students that they are going to learn more about what respect means and how it will help us get along with each other.

INSTRUCTION

Intermediate: You may adapt this instruction to cooperative-group work by asking students to write down their answers, either on a worksheet or blank paper, and then share them with the class.

1. Ask students to brainstorm ways they do not like to be treated by each other and by the teacher in the classroom—for example, when others: touch their things, take cuts in line, call their parent names, are mean, spread rumors. List their statements on the board.

2. For each statement listed, ask students how they would like to be treated: "I want you to ask me if you can touch my things," "Don't cut in line," etc.

3. For each statement listed, ask students how they would want to treat others: "If somebody said he wants to be asked before I touch his things, then I have to ask first," "If she doesn't want me to call her mother names, then I cannot do it," etc.

---

4. "When we treat others the way we would like to be treated, what do we call it?" Elicit the answer: "We call it 'treating each other with respect.'"

APPLICATION

Conduct role-plays that demonstrate three of the ways students do not like to be treated that you listed on the board in Step 1 of the instruction. For each statement, ask students to role-play first the way they do not like to be treated (for example: Student #1 is going to the pencil sharpener and Student #2 makes fun of him). Ask the class how the role-plays demonstrated not showing respect. Then ask students to role-play the way they would like to be treated—the respectful way (for example: Student #2 observes Student #1 but doesn't make fun of him. Ask the class how the scenes demonstrated showing respect.

CLOSURE

Primary: Have the puppet repeat the statement, "Get out of my way! I want to be first in line!" Tell the class that now we know that the puppet was not respectful. Ask, "How could the puppet have been respectful to me?" Ask the students if they think that you and everybody else in the class has the right to be treated with respect. Call on several students to explain what the expectation, "I have the right to be treated with respect in this classroom," means to them.

Intermediate: Remind students that when you grabbed the book, you were not being respectful. Ask students if they think that you and everybody else in the class has the right to be treated with respect. Call on several students to explain what the expectation, "I have the right to be treated with respect in this classroom," means to them. ■

Follow-Up Activity

Make a copy of the "Classroom Pledge" reproducible, or create a large-size poster version of it and have students design a decorative border. Have all students commit themselves to observing the rules for getting along together by signing the pledge. Place the poster where it is visible to all students.

Home Study Activity

Primary: Ask students to draw pictures of how they show respect for others at home and how others show respect for them.

Intermediate: Ask students to write in their journal about situations at home in which they would like to be treated more respectfully, then about situations in which they could improve showing respect for others.

Classroom Pledge

I promise to myself and everyone in this classroom, that I will show respect by treating others the way I would like to be treated.

I will choose to follow the classroom rules for getting along together because I want to help make my school a safe and caring place.

We pledge as a class to do our best to cooperate with each other.

TEACHER AND STUDENT SIGNATURES

_____   _____

_____   _____

_____   _____

_____   _____

_____   _____

_____   _____

_____   _____

_____   _____

_____   _____

_____   _____

_____   _____

_____   _____

_____   _____

_____   _____

Lesson #4

DEALING WITH "PUT-DOWNS"

Let me say that another way.

This lesson and Lesson #3, "Treating Each Other with Respect," teach behavior for two prosocial expectations that are suggested for your classroom.

PRIMARY OUTCOME

Students will be able to identify what "put-downs" are and choose between two alternate behaviors.

MATERIALS NEEDED

Anticipatory Set: Primary—puppet, paper heart

ANTICIPATORY SET

Primary: Have a puppet wear a paper-heart "pin." Give a put-down to the puppet: "That's the ugliest heart pin I ever saw!" The puppet says, "I didn't feel very good when you said that—it sounds like a 'put-down.'" Tell students that they are going to learn more about why put-downs don't help people get along in the classroom, and what they can do about it.

Intermediate: Share a personal story with the class, such as, "When I wore a brand-new shirt the other day, I heard somebody say, 'What a dorky shirt!' My feelings were so hurt when I heard this 'put-down' that I felt just terrible." Tell students that they are going to learn more about why put-downs don't help people get along in the classroom, and what they can do about it.

INSTRUCTION

1. "Give me some examples of put-downs." Elicit responses of put-downs that are spoken aloud, written (as in a note), given in a serious manner, or a joking manner. Write the examples on the board. "These put-downs are words that are used to criticize people or find fault with them."

2. "Sometimes people are just kidding around or teasing each other and are having fun, and then it goes too far, and somebody gives a put-down. Other times people just seem to want to give put-downs to others. Why do you think people give put-downs?" Elicit responses: because they are jealous and want to make a person feel bad; to feel "better" than someone, to act "cool" with friends.

3. "How does it feel to receive a put-down? How does it feel to put others down?"

4. "What could happen if people in this class kept giving put-downs?": There would be bad feelings; it could cause arguments or fights; no one would feel safe, we would not get along.

5. "When you feel like using a put-down, you can make two other choices instead."

- "You can let go. You have the power to let go of the feeling or the thought and walk away. Remind yourself that if you are going to treat the other person with respect, you would not use a put-down."

- "You can put it a better way (or, rephrase). If you feel you must say something, you can think about a better way to say it. Rather than making someone feel bad by making a judgment—'What a stupid sweater'—make an observation—'I have never seen that sweater before.'"

APPLICATION

Have students do role-plays, acting out the scenarios listed below. Ask the players to incorporate a put-down into the scene, then replay it, making the choice to let go or put it a better way.

- A student continually misses a ball while playing handball.

- A student comes to school with torn clothing.

- A student receives a poor grade on a paper.

- When called on, a student misspells an easy word.

CLOSURE

Primary: Tell students there are consequences for themselves and for others when they give a put-down: "Just as the puppet felt hurt when I put down the heart pin, it hurts you too when you receive a put-down. It hurts everybody to receive a put-down. When you have the feeling that you want to give a put-down, what other choices do you have?" Ask for a choral response: "We can. . . 'let go,' or we can. . . 'put it a better way.'"

Intermediate: Tell students there are consequences for themselves and for others when they give a put-down: "Just as I felt bad when I wore my new shirt and heard that put-down, it hurts you too when you receive a put-down. It hurts everybody to receive a put-down. When you have the feeling you want to give a put-down, what other choices do you have?" Ask for a choral response: "We can let go, or we can put it a better way." ■

Follow-Up Activity

Ask students to write about a put-down they have received or that they have witnessed another person receiving. Tell them not to reveal any students' names in their example. Ask them to describe their feelings at the time and what they would have preferred the other person to do instead of giving a put-down. Call on volunteers to share their writing with the class.

Home Study Activity

Intermediate: Ask students to use a dictionary to define the following words: tease, mock, detract, belittle, depreciate, degrade, humiliate, ridicule, condemn, disapprove, criticize. In class, discuss each word as it relates to using put-downs with other people.

CHAPTER 3

Teaching and Reinforcing Prosocial Skills

Like many elementary teachers today, you spend more and more of your time looking for ways to integrate curriculum. Research shows that students learn better when they can see connections among disciplines, so you design teaching units that relate reading, language arts, math, science, and social studies to a common theme.

To have a caring community of learners, you need to add another "discipline" to those you teach: prosocial skills. These are skills that students will need to master in order to meet the prosocial expectations—or rules—for behavior you have determined for your classroom. Teaching students what it means to cooperate, share, listen, negotiate, empathize, problem solve—and what those behaviors look like, sound like, and feel like—is an essential step in helping children learn to get along.

But if you're wondering how you can fit one more topic into an already overcrowded school day, remember your integrated curriculum. The easiest and most effective way to present prosocial skills is to tie them to content-area activities and units you already teach. By doing so, you reinforce positive behaviors daily and give students opportunities to practice these skills again and again.

Teaching Prosocial Skills

In fact, you probably spend more time teaching prosocial skills than you recognize. Take listening, for example. We think of listening as a component of literacy, along with reading, writing, and speaking. But active listening is also a vital social skill. We know how to respond to others by hearing what they have to say and how they say it. When we help students develop their listening skills, we help them enhance their communication and social skills, too.

This chapter is filled with teaching plans for helping younger and older elementary students learn the essential behaviors that help individuals and groups get along:

As you present the lessons, remember to share the purpose and objectives with students.

Identify the skills they'll be learning and why they are important. You want to increase students' awareness of how they interact with one another and why positive interactions help them get along.

Reinforcing Prosocial Skills

So you've taught active listening and taking turns and paying compliments. The students were engaged and the lessons went well. Is the work done? Will you have a newly cooperative, caring class?

You know the answer: not yet. It will take many more opportunities to practice these skills before students begin to use them automatically. It's not enough to teach prosocial skills once. You need to reinforce them by reviewing the behaviors and why each is important.

But that's where your integrated curriculum comes in. There are many ways to tie prosocial skills to daily lessons in other subjects and to your classroom routines. Here are a few ideas to get you started.

- Many stories in your literature series are sure to include situations that involve conflict. As you discuss each story, talk with students about how the characters got along, how they solved their disagreements, and what they could have done differently to avoid conflict. Encourage students to relate the characters' experiences to their own lives.

- When studying social studies concepts related to communities and civic rules and laws, make comparisons to your classroom community. Talk about how communities help their citizens get along. Relate setting rules and laws in communities to the prosocial expectations for your classroom.

- Use real or hypothetical conflict situations as opportunities to help students develop problem-solving and critical-thinking skills.

- As you study wars and other conflicts in history, talk about how conflicts between groups of people or nations are like conflicts between individuals. What causes conflict? What are better alternatives to violence in solving conflicts?

- As you study how the human body works in science, talk about how our bodies react when we are angry. For example there is increased blood flow to the face, and the heart pounds. Explain the fight or flight response to a threatening situation. Help students recognize that how we use our ears, eyes, mouth, hands, feet, and brains to get along with others is in our control. For example, our ears allow us to hear, but we have to consciously *listen* to others in order to communicate effectively.

- Use holiday observations to reinforce prosocial skills. For example, design a Thanksgiving bulletin board that asks students to write sentences or poems of thanks for having great classmates. On Valentine's Day, invite children to make valentines with compliments for classmates.

- Throughout the day, use lots of praise to positively reinforce appropriate interactions between students. When students share, take turns, compliment others, listen carefully to others, praise them! Don't miss an opportunity to cite a student for demonstrating appropriate behavior. You'll find that praise is a powerful motivator in helping students remember and use prosocial skills.

- Give students awards, such as the reproducibles on pages 160 and 161. Students take pride in having tangible evidence of their appropriate behavior. Awards such as these often end up as treasured childhood keepsakes.

Reinforcing prosocial skills need not be difficult, and in fact, it can be fun. Once you start looking for ways to promote prosocial skills, you'll notice that many of the activities and routines you've always done with students have valuable social skills at heart. The difference now is that students are acquiring a growing awareness of the behaviors that promote positive interactions. Increase their understanding by consistently pointing out how they are developing particular skills for getting along with each other.

Using Redirecting Techniques

Another valuable way to help students remember getting-along skills is through redirecting techniques. They allow you to correct a student's inappropriate behavior without having to issue a consequence. Here are three successful approaches to redirecting a student who is not sharing or listening to others, for instance.

- *Physical proximity:* Walk over and stand by the student. Your presence will be a signal to the child that you're aware of his or her inappropriate behavior.
- *Saying the student's name:* "Suppose Georgio was in a car traveling at 40 miles an hour from New York to Boston." Just saying the student's name will often correct the misbehavior.
- *Praising appropriate behavior:* Praise students who are sharing or listening attentively. "Emily, I like the way you're

sharing the markers with Adele." This focuses everyone's attention on the desired prosocial behavior.

Redirecting techniques should be used with students who exhibit minor behavioral infractions. When a student's antisocial behavior is more serious, you'll want to demonstrate that you mean business by imposing consequences.

Using Modeling to Reinforce Prosocial Behavior

Not all of the methods you use to teach and reinforce prosocial skills will involve direct instruction. One of the most effective ways you can promote these positive interactions is through your own actions. You, as well as other significant adults in children's lives, are powerful role models. Although you can't control the kind of models students have in their parents and other relatives, you can control the prosocial model they have in you.

There are two areas in particular that you can model for students every day:

- Attentive listening.
- Paying compliments.

Modeling Attentive Listening

Students talk to you all day long. You have countless opportunities to show students how to be good listeners. Start by communicating to children that you care about what they have to say and that you attentively listen to their every word. Demonstrate the body language of good listening:

- Turn or lean toward the speaker.
- Make eye contact.

- Nod to signal that you're with the speaker.
- Don't interrupt.

(Keep in mind that attentive listening techniques in classrooms may be different from those in certain cultural communities. For example, in many diverse communities, interrupting and no eye contact may be seen as respectful and attentive.)

Sure, you may be thinking, but I'm the teacher. I'm busy. I can't always give each student speaking to me my undivided attention. And besides, I can listen and correct a paper or write an assignment on the chalkboard at the same time.

Granted, the demands placed on a teacher by a room full of lively first-graders or intense 10-year-olds are great. It's *not* always possible to give every child your undivided attention. But consider the message you send students when you turn your back on them and write on the board when they're telling you something that is important to them. Think about the kind of listener you present to them.

Throughout the day, make your goal one of modeling how to listen whenever a student or another adult speaks to you.

Paying Compliments

Children being children, it's fairly easy to slip into a negative mode in the classroom. We can spend the day saying "no . . . not now . . . don't do that . . . no talking . . . stop that . . . " and on and on. Of course, sometimes those "no" words are necessary to maintain classroom discipline. But just as important is paying compliments to the students who are on task, who get along with others, who meet our prosocial expectations.

Model giving compliments to students: "Nice job, Andrea." "Thank you for helping out, Hakeem." "I like that new shirt, José." "Great game, Barbara." If praising children and paying compliments doesn't come naturally to you—and in truth, it doesn't to many of us—stick a "remember to praise" Post-it™ on lesson notes or jot down a reminder inside your plan book.

When you show students how to give compliments, they're more likely to compliment others. But if the model you offer students is negative, if you demonstrate that you're more focused on what's wrong than on what's right, you're just as likely to see the same negative attitude in your students.

No teacher is perfect, and there will be times when you will not be the ideal model of prosocial behavior. You're only human. But remembering your power as a role model may help you to stop and think about whether you are demonstrating for students the behaviors you want to see from them, and how you can enhance your own prosocial skills.

Using Teachable Moments to Reinforce Prosocial Skills

Closely tied to your ability as a role model to influence students' behaviors is the impact of children's own demonstrations of prosocial skills. Be on the lookout for opportunities to help all students learn from a peer's actions.

Why do we look for and value teachable moments in other subjects? Because we recognize that these incidents and events have special meaning for children. They come out of students' own experiences, not some abstract textbook example. That's why a teachable moment is often the breakthrough in concept development for some students. It's the moment when they really "get it." True understanding of human interaction can also occur in your classroom when you make use of teachable moments to promote positive social skills.

Teachable Moments Are Everywhere

A sharp-eyed teacher will see and hear many helping and caring behaviors to offer up to the group. Here's an example:

> The class is on the playground after lunch. Roberta and Soo-Yi are playfully chasing one another when Roberta takes a tumble. Before you have time to cross the playground, Evan and Kamal, digging in the dirt nearby, go to Roberta's assistance. Soo-Yi also runs back to check on her friend. Roberta is unhurt and thanks Evan, Kamal, and Soo-Yi for making sure she's okay.

This is a wonderful incident to bring to the whole class's attention. Once everyone is back inside, let all four children tell in their own words what happened. Encourage Roberta to share how she felt when she realized her friends were watching out for her. Ask Evan, Kamal, and Soo-Yi to recall what they were thinking when they went to Roberta's aid. Encourage the class to describe qualities their peers demonstrated: caring, compassion, sympathy, concern.

Spotlighting students' positive interactions has another benefit, and it gets to the heart of human nature. You know that most children crave attention. Many students quickly learn at home and at school that they can get more attention if they act out. When you accent positive interactions and praise demonstrations

of cooperation and caring among students, you give your attention-seekers a compelling reason to act appropriately. When you use teachable moments to communicate the behaviors you want to see, you increase the likelihood that you'll see more of those actions from more students.

Turn to "Great Ideas: Promoting Friendship" on page 65 for activities that will help students explore what it means to be a friend and how using the prosocial skills they have learned in this chapter will help them be a better friend to others.

Not Just School Skills, Life Skills

Prosocial skills empower students to get along. They are foundation skills that lay the groundwork for a more harmonious classroom. But more than that, they are life skills that every person needs to be a happy, healthy, productive human being. You cannot create a caring community of students without teaching prosocial skills. And we as educators cannot help shape future citizens who will build caring families and caring companies and caring towns and cities without putting the teaching of prosocial skills high on our own list of priorities.

Take the Time to Teach Prosocial Skills

Many of my first-graders don't know how to relate to other children. They are very self-centered and have a difficult time cooperating, sharing, taking turns, or displaying empathy for others. When they don't get their way, they punch, hit, shove, and call each other names.

Although in 22 years of teaching I've always had some children with these kinds of problems in getting along with others, I have many more of them today.

So I begin the year by setting prosocial expectations for my students, such as "Listen without interrupting"; "No put-downs"; "Keep hands and feet to yourself." Then I actively teach what those rules mean, along with the social skills that children need to get along, using puppets and discussion. And I reinforce, and reinforce, and reinforce. I look for teachable moments to praise students for sharing, taking turns, or other helping behaviors.

When children have conflicts, I bring the pair who were fighting together and I guide them in talking about what happened. My goal is to help students recognize that their actions affect others' feelings. Children need the chance to say, "You made me feel bad." Both students need to think about what they could do differently next time to avoid a conflict.

As the primary-level chairperson in my building, I work with new teachers and I emphasize the importance of teaching students to get along. Quite simply, you can't teach academic skills if you don't take the time to teach children to listen and cooperate. I tell first-year teachers that they'll spend all of their time drying tears and settling disputes if they don't set clear rules for how students will treat each other. Sure, children will test the behavior boundaries, but I firmly believe they want to know the boundaries are there.

So many students come from homes where behavior expectations are not in force. Many children have never been taught good manners or how to share. But children *can* learn these skills. They do every year in my classroom!

Alice Amick, Field Elementary
Mesa, Arizona

Lesson #5

USING GOOD MANNERS

Thank you for being my teacher.

PRIMARY OUTCOME

Students will be able to use the words and actions of being polite and respectful.

MATERIALS NEEDED

Anticipatory Set: Snack food

Follow-Up Activity: "Good Manners Word Puzzle" reproducible, page 41

Home Study Activity: "Having Good Manners Helps Us Get Along with Each Other" reproducible, page 42

ANTICIPATORY SET

Walk into the classroom and distribute a small snack (cookie, fruit or pretzel) to each student. Then say: "I counted ___ students who said 'Thank you.' I really feel good when you say thank you. It shows me you appreciated what I did, and you used words that were polite. You had good manners, which we're going to learn more about today."

INSTRUCTION

1. Define "good manners."

   • Primary: Tell students, "'Good manners' are polite ways of behaving. Being polite to people shows respect for them. People with good manners say 'Please' and 'Thank you.'"

   • Intermediate: Have students look up the words "manners" and "polite" in a dictionary, then write the

definitions on the board. Ask for examples of words and phrases that are considered polite. Say that the way in which polite words are said is as important as the words themselves. Give an example by saying "Thank you" three different ways: angrily, politely and sincerely.

2. "We can show good manners in two ways: with our words and with our actions. First, what words would we use to be polite to someone?" Elicit from students the words of showing good manners: please, thank you, you're welcome, may I, excuse me, I'm sorry, hello, goodbye.

3. Next, elicit from students the actions of showing good manners and the words that might accompany them: assisting others ("I would like to help you"); greeting a new student (shake hands and say, "It's nice to meet you"); making sure everybody gets a snack you are handing out in the classroom.

4. "Does it help us to get along with each other if we show good manners to just a few people in our classroom?" Explain: "People who have good manners use them with everybody; it shows we care about people."

5. Present several situations and ask students to use the words and actions

of showing good manners.

- "You meet someone for the first time. What would you say or do?": "I would shake hands and say 'Nice to meet you.'"

- "You broke your friend's toy by mistake. What would you say or do?": "I would say, 'I'm sorry.'"

- "You wanted to use your friend's red marker and it was laying on the table. Would you just take it?": "I would say, 'May I please borrow your red marker.'"

6. "How will using manners and being polite help us to get along with each other in our classroom?" Elicit responses: prevent bad feelings, arguments and fights; people would be more helpful; make people feel good; have a happier classroom. Refer to previous concepts learned by saying, "Using good manners means we are treating other people with respect."

APPLICATION

Ask students to role-play using good manners, through both words and actions, in situations such as the following:

- You introduce a new student to the class and ask two students to come up and escort the new student to a desk and act as guides for the day.

- A visitor comes into the classroom and says, "Hello, class," then leaves and says, "Goodbye. It was nice to have visited with you."

- A student is trying to carry a heavy stack of books.

Intermediate: Ask students to role-play in groups first not using good manners, then using good manners in situations such as the previous ones. After the role-plays are completed, say, "Using good manners not only shows respect for people, people respect you for using them. If you practice using good manners, it will become a habit that will earn you respect throughout your life."

CLOSURE

Walk throughout the classroom as you did earlier and distribute another small snack. Then say, "I counted ___ students who said 'Thank you.' You're welcome. I am happy to give this snack to you. This class knows how to use good manners!" ∎

Follow-Up Activity

Intermediate Activity #1: Give each student a copy of the "Good Manners Word Puzzle." Have students complete the word search in their small groups, then together use a dictionary to define any words they don't understand. Have a classwide discussion on the meaning of the words and how they relate to having good manners.

Intermediate Activity #2: Discuss with students what is considered good manners in their families or in other cultures or geographic areas.

Home Study Activity

Give each student a copy of the "Having Good Manners Helps Us Get Along with Each Other" reproducible. Have students draw pictures or cartoons showing how using good manners helps people get along. Parents of younger students may record the story on the back of the drawing ("This is a picture of me at the dinner table saying 'Please pass the bread.'")

Good Manners
Word Puzzle

R	E	S	U	C	G	G	R	P	E	N	D	U
E	R	O	P	I	I	R	S	O	P	R	U	M
C	E	C	P	U	S	E	A	L	O	M	C	A
T	F	I	L	O	I	E	Z	C	L	A	O	N
C	I	E	E	S	L	T	G	I	I	N	N	N
I	N	T	A	C	T	I	R	T	T	O	D	E
C	E	Y	S	O	T	N	A	R	E	S	U	R
U	D	R	E	R	E	G	A	R	D	Y	C	S
L	C	E	V	D	R	E	S	P	E	C	T	E
T	O	F	C	I	V	I	L	I	T	Y	C	P
U	U	I	T	A	I	N	E	C	I	O	U	S
R	R	W	E	L	C	O	M	E	E	O	U	S
E	C	O	U	R	T	E	O	U	S	A	R	G

FIND THESE WORDS:

POLITE	RESPECT	CULTURE	PLEASE
COURTEOUS	CIVILITY	TACT	GRACIOUS
MANNERS	REGARD	CORDIAL	REFINED
GREETING	WELCOME	SOCIETY	CONDUCT

Having Good Manners
Helps Us Get Along with Each Other

Draw a picture or a cartoon showing how having good manners
helps us to get along with each other.

Compliments for You and Me

I like you.

You look nice.

I'm glad we're friends.

I like working with you.

You're fun.

I'd like to get to know you better.

You're a good buddy.

Congratulations for…

Thank you for sharing…

I like the way you look.

You're super at…

I'm glad we're friends.

I wish you a wonderful day.

Thank you for teaching me something new today.

I appreciate your help.

Thanks for including me.

You are a kind person.

You're funny.

It's nice to see you in school every day.

You are dependable.

You're a great listener.

You are very creative.

I like it when you…

I'm happy to know you.

Good job.

I'm proud of you because…

You are special…

I like it when you smile…

You're my special friend.

I'm glad you are in our class.

You are a caring person.

You are very helpful.

I enjoy being with you.

How nice of you to do that.

I think you are terrific.

I hope you do well. You deserve it.

You give the best compliments.

I especially appreciated it when you…

I'm glad you're in my group.

You're fun to know.

Your clothes look great!

I feel good when I'm with you.

You made me laugh.

I like to sit with you.

You are a great friend.

I like playing with you.

You're a good buddy.

I like your…

I'm glad I know you.

You are so smart.

I like the way you…

You look very nice.

You are a great helper.

I appreciate your help.

You're so good in sports.

You're the best!

You Deserve a Compliment!

To: _____

From: _____

You Deserve a Compliment!

To: _____

From: _____

You Deserve a Compliment!

To: _____

From: _____

You Deserve a Compliment!

To: _____

From: _____

LISTENING TO ENHANCE COMMUNICATION

Part One: Listening Attentively

This is very interesting.

PRIMARY OUTCOME

Students will be able to demonstrate and practice attentive listening skills to help them communicate effectively.

MATERIALS NEEDED

None

ANTICIPATORY SET

"How many of you like to listen to someone tell a really good story? How many of you think you are good listeners when someone tells you a really good story? Excellent. That means you are what we call 'attentive listeners.'" You are going to learn more today about how important it is to listen attentively, and how listening to each other will help us get along together better in our classroom."

INSTRUCTION

1. "Why is it important to listen?" Elicit responses: to get ideas, share information, get directions, find out what someone needs or how someone feels.

2. "What do we do with our voices when we are listening?" Elicit responses and list on the board:
   - Keep voices quiet.
   - Do not interrupt.

3. "We can also show we are listening by what we do with our body. We call this 'body language.'" Elicit from students what the body language of good listening is and list on the board:
   - Turn and lean toward the speaker.
   - Make eye contact.
   - Nod your head to signal that you are listening.

4. Elicit from students what would happen if they used good-listening habits—such as not interrupting and positive body language—with other students in the classroom:
   - The person who speaks would feel good that you were paying attention, and feel respected.
   - The person who listens might learn something new from the speaker. The person who listens attentively has good manners and shows respect for the speaker.

   "When we listen and are listened to, it helps us get along better in our classroom."

APPLICATION

Pair up students and say one of them is to be the speaker and the other will be the listener. Ask the speaker to tell a really good story (suggest some stories: favorite movie, book or television show, fairy tale, personal experience) and tell the listener to practice good-listening skills. After two minutes, ask them to switch roles. When the role-play is completed, ask students to describe their feelings about being both the speaker and the listener when listening attentively.

CLOSURE

Have students repeat chorally the guidelines for attentive listening that you listed on the board. ■

Follow-Up Activity

Help students understand how difficult it can be to communicate clearly sometimes by conducting the original "telephone" game: Whisper a short, simple message into a student's ear and ask that the message be whispered from student to student. Ask the last student to repeat the message aloud and see if it concurs with your original statement. For intermediate students, say that they are going to be learning (in Part Two, "Listening Actively") how to improve their communication and what they can do to make sure they have heard correctly what someone has said.

Home Study Activity

Have students write a few paragraphs about times when it is important to listen to each other at home and the reasons why it is important.

Lesson #8

LISTENING TO ENHANCE COMMUNICATION

Part Two: Listening Actively

You are glad because I listened to you.

This lesson is recommended for intermediate students.

PRIMARY OUTCOME

Students will demonstrate active listening skills to help them communicate with each other more effectively.

MATERIALS NEEDED

Application: "Active Listening: Speaker's Checklist" reproducible, page 51

ANTICIPATORY SET

"We talked before about how you listen attentively when someone tells you a story: You don't interrupt and you use certain body language to show you're listening. It's a quiet way of listening. Another way to listen to people is to listen 'actively.' When you listen actively, you are not quiet—you tell the speaker that you heard and understood what he or she said. It is very helpful to listen actively when there is a problem or disagreement between you and another person because if you understand each other, you have a better chance of solving the problem."

INSTRUCTION

1. "As we have said, if there is a problem between you and another person, that's an especially good time to listen actively. There are other times too that you can use active listening to help you understand another person better:

if you don't understand what someone said, or if someone is being emotional—sad, angry or happy. Here's how you listen actively." (List the three steps of active listening on the board as you present them.)

2. Step 1: "Repeat what you heard." Tell students that when the speaker has finished talking, the listener repeats what the speaker said so that both can make sure the listener understood it. Have students practice this technique. Make several statements, such as "You always tell Yuki lies about me." Ask students to be the listeners and repeat what you said: "You said that I always tell Yuki lies about you."

3. Step 2: "Rephrase what you heard." Model this technique by being the listener and rephrasing one of your statements: "You think that I am telling lies about you to Yuki." Ask students to rephrase your other statements as well. (Variation: As the speaker, give a lengthier description about a special event, trip or game and ask the listener to rephrase it by giving just the main idea in his or her own words.)

4. Step 3: "Acknowledge the feelings as well as the words of the other

person." As the speaker, repeat the statement, "You always tell Yuki lies about me." Call on students to rephrase the statement showing they understand you feelings: "You are really angry because you think I am telling Yuki lies about you."

5. Ask students how they would respond, using the active-listening technique, in other conflict situations: A student says, "I saw you take my book and I want it back!" (Listener: "You believe I took your book and you would like it returned. You're angry about it.") A student says, "I hate it when you bump into me all the time. Why can't you look where you're going!" (Listener: "You're upset because you think I'm not being careful and always bumping into you.")

6. "We listen actively to make sure we understand each other, and when we understand each other, it helps us to get along better."

APPLICATION

As you did in Part One of this lesson, pair up students and say that one of them is to be the speaker and the other the listener. Ask the speakers to say a sentence or two about something exciting, upsetting, scary or sad that happened to them recently. Tell the listeners: "This time you will be active listeners. First repeat the speaker's sentence just as you heard it. Then rephrase it in your own words and say if the speaker seemed happy, angry or sad or had some other feeling." After two minutes, have the speaker fill out the "Active Listening" checklist and ask the partners to switch roles. When the role-

play is completed, ask students to discuss the results of their checklists and describe their feelings about being a speaker and a listener when using active listening.

CLOSURE

Have students in small groups write the rules for good listening. Post the charts around the classroom. Explain that listening is not just about keeping quiet, it is also about showing the other person that you heard what the person said and understood how the person felt. Say that in the classroom, students can use listening attentively and listening actively in the following situations to show they are good listeners:

• When someone is teaching. (attentively)

• When something good happens. (actively)

• When a student disagrees with someone. (actively) ■

Follow-Up Activity

Have students work in small groups to come up with a list of reasons why it could be important to listen actively to others in school. Ask each group to share its list with the class.

Home Study Activity

Ask students to draw a cartoon in two panels showing two persons interacting. One person is the speaker and the other the listener who is listening actively. The first panel shows the speaker talking and the listener repeating the speaker's words. The second panel shows the listener rephrasing the words and acknowledging the speakers feelings. Students can write the dialogue in dialogue "balloons."

Active Listening

SPEAKER'S CHECKLIST

To the speaker: Complete the checklist.

Speaker's Name _____

Listener's Name _____

Did the listener:	Yes	No
Repeat what the speaker said?	☐	☐
Rephrase what the speaker said?	☐	☐
Acknowledge the speaker's feelings?	☐	☐

Active Listening

SPEAKER'S CHECKLIST

To the speaker: Complete the checklist.

Speaker's Name _____

Listener's Name _____

Did the listener:	Yes	No
Repeat what the speaker said?	☐	☐
Rephrase what the speaker said?	☐	☐
Acknowledge the speaker's feelings?	☐	☐

UNDERSTANDING OUR FEELINGS

It's all right to have feelings.

Before students can be expected to express their feelings constructively, they must be aware of their feelings. Therefore, this lesson, "Understanding Our Feelings," is a prerequisite for two other lessons in this book:

- *Lesson #10, "Using 'I Messages,'" which teaches intermediate-level students how to express their feelings in a prosocial manner.*

- *Lesson #13, "Setting Expectations for Getting Along in a Community Circle," which establishes a safe environment for students to express feelings.*

PRIMARY OUTCOME

Students will be able to demonstrate a variety of feelings and be able to recognize others' feelings.

MATERIALS NEEDED

Anticipatory Set: Magazine or newspaper cutouts of people showing different expressions on their faces.

Application and Home Study Activity: "These Are My Feelings" reproducible, page 55

Follow-Up Activity: "What Feelings Do I Have?" reproducible, page 56

ANTICIPATORY SET

Show students pictures of people with different expressions, and ask students to guess how the people are feeling. Then say, "Even though these people didn't say anything, you guessed how they might be feeling. Everybody has feelings. They are normal human emotions. It is very important that we understand our feelings, and others' feelings too, because it will help us understand each other and get along better."

INSTRUCTION

1. "Feelings are messages that tell us what is happening inside of us. Some feelings are comfortable and some are uncomfortable." Elicit from students as many feelings as possible and list them on the board under the two categories—for example, "Comfortable": excited, happy, proud, lovable, hopeful; "Uncomfortable": angry, sad, disappointed, ashamed.

2. "When you have comfortable feelings, how might you show them to other people?" Elicit responses: smile, laugh, be friendly, hug, be calm, have energy. "Is it hard to show your comfortable feelings? How do you think it affects others when we show our comfortable feelings?"

3. "When you have uncomfortable feelings, how might you show them?" Elicit responses: frown, tremble, sweat, fast heartbeat, cry, yell, hit. "Is

it hard to show your uncomfortable feelings? How do you think it affects others when we show our uncomfortable feelings?"

4. "Do you ever have feelings you are afraid to express? How do you feel inside when you have feelings you are afraid to express?" Elicit responses: feel worse, more afraid, more tense, angrier; hurt more; might get a stomach ache, headache; might cry a lot.

5. "It is okay to have feelings—all kinds of feelings. You have told me that sometimes when you show feelings you might hurt others, or that you might even be afraid to show your feelings. In this class, you will be learning some good ways to show or express your feelings—ways that won't hurt others or yourself. How do you think showing or expressing our feelings might help us to get along with each other better?" Elicit responses: feel more connected to others; understand each other better; lead to better communication; better chance to work out problems.

APPLICATION

Using a copy of the "These Are My Feelings" reproducible, cut all or some of the words into separate pieces and place them in a box or jar titled "Everybody Has Feelings." (Choose the words that are appropriate for your grade level.) Ask students to draw a "feeling" from the box and act it out without saying aloud what the feeling is, and see if the class can guess the feeling. After each

demonstration, ask if anyone has ever felt that way. After the activity is completed, say "We can see that people have all kinds of feelings, and that it is normal to have them."

CLOSURE

"You have learned that it is okay to have feelings, but that sometimes the way we feel leads us to say or do things that might hurt other people, or might even hurt you. In this class, you will be learning how to show your feelings in a way that doesn't hurt anybody and will even help us get along better with each other." ■

Follow-Up Activity

Give each student a copy of the "What Feelings Do I Have?" reproducible. Tell them to think about the different feelings they have inside of them. (You can give students a copy of the "These Are My Feelings" reproducible to stimulate their thinking.) Ask them to fill in the first column with the feelings they have often, and the second column with the feelings they think they have never felt. Call on students to share their responses in each column. Point out again how their responses show that everybody has feelings and that they vary from person to person.

Home Study Activity

Give each student a copy of the "These Are My Feelings" reproducible to take home. Ask them to write about a situation outside of school in which they experienced one of these feelings. Primary students can draw a picture.

These Are My Feelings

excited	important	funny
sad	concerned	hungry
lonely	tired	gentle
sorry	grief	confident
frightened	left out	furious
hurt	impatient	embarrassed
silly	content	surprised
confused	caring	ashamed
quiet	cool	anxious
jealous	strong	worried
angry	loud	frustrated
disappointed	sassy	hopeless
nervous	upset	loving
proud	bored	humiliated
happy	unimportant	alone
loved	weak	suspicious
energetic	joyful	annoyed

What Feelings Do I Have?

Feelings I Have Often	Feelings I Think I Have Never Felt
_____	_____
_____	_____
_____	_____
_____	_____
_____	_____
_____	_____
_____	_____
_____	_____
_____	_____
_____	_____
_____	_____
_____	_____
_____	_____
_____	_____
_____	_____

USING "I MESSAGES"

> *I feel proud when I can say what I need.*

This lesson is recommended for intermediate students.

PRIMARY OUTCOME

Students will be able to use "I messages" in order to facilitate communication in a conflict situation.

MATERIALS NEEDED

Anticipatory Set: Radio or tape player

Application: "Using an 'I Message'" reproducible, page 59

ANTICIPATORY SET

Select some music on the radio (or tape player) and turn up the volume so it is loud. When everyone is quiet, lower the volume and say, "Let's pretend that a person who wanted to hear music turned on this radio very loud. I want to tell the person that it bothers me to hear such loud music. We want two different things, don't we? When people disagree like that, we call it conflict. Many times you or I will disagree with another person—have a conflict. It's normal. We can't always agree with every single thing every person says or does. To help prevent disagreements from getting worse, there are things we can do. We can speak to the person we disagree with in a way that can help us solve the disagreement and get along better. It's called giving an 'I message' and we're going to learn what it means and how to do it."

INSTRUCTION

1. "We've talked about how important it is to be able to express our feelings to other people. When something happens that you don't feel good about—something that you don't like—it's okay to tell a person that it bothers you. There are two ways to describe how you feel about something. You can use a 'You message' or you can use an 'I message.'"

   - "A 'You message' is when you tell a person: *You* make me so mad; *You* give me my pencil back; *You* always do this to me. You are saying that you choose to blame the other person for something."

   - An 'I message' is when you tell a person: *I* don't like something; *I* need something, *I* have feelings about something. You are saying, *I* choose not to blame you for anything; *I* am responsible for my own feelings."

2. "When the person played the loud music on the radio, I could have said, 'You are making so much noise you are giving me a headache, so you had better turn down that radio.' Would that have been an *I* message or a *You* message? If I had said, 'I would like you to turn down that radio because I am bothered when it is

loud.' Is that an *I* message or a *You* message? Which way might make the disagreement worse? Which way might make the disagreement better?"

3. Ask students to brainstorm a list of conflict situations they encounter frequently and list them on the board. Guide several students to respond to two or three of the situations with a "You message." Ask what could happen to the disagreement when that kind of message is given.

4. "Now let's learn how to give an 'I message.'" List guidelines on the board:
   - I feel (name the feeling). . .
   - When you (state the problem). . . .
   - I would like (say what you want to happen to make things better). . . .

   Ask individual students to respond to the same conflict situations they chose earlier (in Step #3) with an "I message" instead of a "You message." Ask what could happen to the disagreement when an "I message" is given.

5. "If a conflict like one of these happened to you, which kind of message would you want to use to get along better with the other person—a 'You message' or an 'I message'?"

6. "When someone gives you an 'I message,' that person is telling you about his or her feelings, and it is important to respect and accept that person's feelings. If you need to show your own feelings to that person, you can use an 'I message' too."

APPLICATION

Give each student a copy of the "Using an 'I Message'" reproducible. Have students in small groups choose one of the other conflict situations from the list created in Step #3. Ask them to decide how they would deal with the problem and then fill out the worksheet. Have students practice the results with their group.

CLOSURE

"If something happens that you don't like or that you disagree with in this classroom, use can use an 'I message' to tell the person your feelings. You do not have to get into a fight, you do not have to be quiet and not say anything, and you do not have to ask for the teacher's help. You can use an 'I message' to help you and the other person start talking together about the problem." ■

Follow-Up Activity

Students in small groups create posters with the "I message" steps (I feel; when you; I would like) using words and pictures. Place the posters in the classroom for future reference.

Home Study Activity

Using current events information from TV, the newspaper or the radio, have students rewrite a story/event with the characters solving conflicts using "I messages." They can create a cartoon with three panels. The statements in the first panel begin with "I feel," the second panel with "When you," and the third panel with "I would like."

Using an "I Message"

Problem: _____

_____

_____

"I Message":

I feel: _____

_____

When: _____

_____

I would like: _____

_____

Name _____

Using an "I Message"

Problem: _____

_____

_____

"I Message":

I feel: _____

_____

When: _____

_____

I would like: _____

_____

Lesson #11

SHARING AND TAKING TURNS

When I share, it shows I care about you.

PRIMARY OUTCOME

Students will be able to share and take turns when working or playing together.

MATERIALS NEEDED

Anticipatory Set: Primary—puppet or stuffed animal, book; Intermediate—magazine

Application: Primary—crayons and paper; Intermediate—markers and paper

ANTICIPATORY SET

Primary: Using a puppet, create a dramatization in which the puppet wants to read the same book you are reading. "What could happen when two people want the same thing. They might fight and tear up the book and then feel bad about each other. We have learned how to use 'I messages' when we disagree with something. There is something else we can do too. When people both want something, we can either share it or take turns with it."

Intermediate: Bring in a magazine that you know is popular with students. "How many of you would like to read this magazine right now?" Depending on the number of responses, say "Hmm. The problem is there is only one magazine and ___ people who want to read it." Tear pages out of the magazine and give them to students. "Was that a good solution? Why not?" Elicit responses: can't read the whole thing, magazine ruined, bad feelings because somebody else got the part you wanted. "When people want the same thing, a better solution would be to share it or take turns with it."

INSTRUCTION

1. "What things have to be shared in this classroom?" Elicit responses: toys, books, classroom equipment, playground equipment, art supplies, computers, teacher's time.

2. "Why do we need to share things in this classroom?" Elicit responses: not enough materials or toys to go around.

3. "Sometimes a person may want something so much that the person just takes it and forgets that it could make the other person feel bad or that it could lead to a fight. Do you always feel like sharing?" Ask for responses and say that you know it's not always easy to share something with another person.

4. "What are some of the things that could happen when people don't want to share?" Elicit responses: bad words and feelings, fights, destruction of property and of friendships.

5. "Because we don't want violence to happen or people to feel bad, we can share things. What are some of the good things that could happen when people share?" Elicit responses: more than one person gets to use something, people don't feel hurt, nobody argues, people get along better.

6. What are some ways can we share things?" Elicit responses: take turns by using a timer or flipping a coin; split something in two; play "rock, paper, scissors" or "one potato, two potato"; do something together (use a puzzle, jump rope). List the solutions on the board. "You can share by using a lot of these ideas. First try to figure out by yourselves how to share. If you can't decide what to do, then you can ask the teacher to help you find a solution."

APPLICATION

Form groups of three and give each group two crayons (or markers) and three pieces of paper. Ask the groups to brainstorm ways to share so that each person can use a crayon. Have the groups practice their solutions by having each person in the group write or illustrate each one they think of on his or her paper using one of the crayons. Discuss the groups' solutions to the problem.

CLOSURE

"Even though we didn't have enough crayons (markers) to go around, look at the great solutions you thought of. And the result is that everyone is getting along in this classroom. In the next 24 hours, look for an opportunity to share something—in class, on the yard, or at home. Use one of the ways to share that we learned, and come back to class and report on it." ■

Follow-Up Activity

Pair up students and tell them they are going to have a 15-minute "Be Fair and Share" time. Give to each set of partners one item such as a book, toy, puzzle, gadget, marker and paper. Tell the partners to discuss as many ways as they can think of to share the item. Then give them 10 minutes to share it. Call on partners to tell the class all the solutions they brainstormed, and if the solution they decided on was satisfactory.

Home Study Activity

Have students list three things they have to share at home with family members— for example, tangible items such as toys, games or books; TV time; chores; bedroom; time with a parent. Ask them to write a paragraph on how they settle each situation.

Lesson #12

DISPLAYING EMPATHY

Note: This lesson is recommended for intermediate students.

PRIMARY OUTCOME

Students will be able to use words and actions that demonstrate sensitivity to others' feelings and thoughts.

MATERIALS NEEDED

Anticipatory Set and Application: Shoes

ANTICIPATORY SET

Bring in several pairs of shoes that could indicate a story behind them—old shoes, running shoes, hiking boots, ballet slippers, rain boots, ski boots, dress-up shoes, dancing shoes, sandals, slippers. Ask students, "What might I be feeling if I were the person wearing these shoes?" Elicit "feeling" responses: tired, excited, happy. "You really understood how I might feel if I were wearing these shoes. You had 'empathy' for me. Empathy means being able to understand and care about other people's feelings—to put yourself in someone else's shoes. You are going to learn three ways to show that you have empathy for someone."

INSTRUCTION

1. "What is 'empathy'?"
   - Primary: Tell students, "Empathy is when a person understands and cares how another person feels about something."

   - Intermediate: Have students use a dictionary to look up the meaning, then call on students to share their definitions.

2. "Why is it a good idea to show empathy? Showing people empathy tells them that they're not alone—that someone understands how they feel, accepts how they feel, respects how they feel, and cares how they feel. We show people empathy. . ."
   - "When good things happen to them—for example, when we're excited about something they did—and they need to know someone cares and that they're not alone."
   - "When bad things happen to them and they need to know that someone cares, and that they're not alone."

3. "When are the best opportunities for people to show empathy—to show they understand someone else's feelings?"
   - Elicit responses for when something good happens: good grade, selected for team, new family member.
   - Elicit responses for when something bad happens: not invited to a party, lost a pet, last one to be selected.

4. "How can we show empathy?":
   - With words. Elicit examples: "You lost your pet; I'm sorry you feel sad." "You must have missed your friends when your family moved."
   - With the way you look and sound. Elicit meaning: The expression on your face and the tone of your voice has to match the words (sad, excited, angry).
   - With actions. Elicit examples: Put your hand on somebody's shoulder. Ask someone to play. Write a friendship note or a birthday card.

5. Have students discuss how they might handle "being in someone else's shoes" and showing empathy during a situation they have encountered—for example, when a new student came to class, when a student was hurt, or when a student was elected an officer of the class.

APPLICATION

Divide students into small groups and give each group a pair of the shoes you used in the beginning of the lesson. Ask each group to make up a story about who wore these shoes and what the person might have been feeling—for example: "These hiking boots were worn by the first woman to climb Mt. Everest. Because she trained so had and so long to accomplish this, she felt happy, excited—and tired!" Have each group select one person to tell the story to the class. Call on students to "put themselves in the other person's shoes" by demonstrating empathy for the person in the story with words, looks or actions.

CLOSURE

"Showing empathy toward another person says that we understand how it feels to 'be in that person's shoes.' It shows we care and helps us to get along with the person. Now that you know what empathy means and how to show it, describe some situations in which you can use this skill." ■

Follow-Up Activity

Have students write short stories or draw pictures using the following words: empathy, caring, understanding, feelings, support, community, friends. Call on students to share the results with the class.

Home Study Activity

Ask students to "put yourself in someone else's shoes" by thinking about a situation with a family member in which the student could have displayed empathy for something that happened. Students can draw cartoons depicting the situation and the words and actions that express empathy.

Promoting Friendship

"Promoting Friendship" is a collection of positive activities that incorporate the use of the prosocial skills taught in this book. The purpose is to make students aware that using the skills and expectations for getting along they learned in previous lessons will help them to make and keep friends. Adapt the activities to the age level of your students, and use the activities at different times during the year to keep alive the premise of friends bonding through the use of prosocial behavior.

FRIENDSHIP HELPERS BULLETIN BOARD

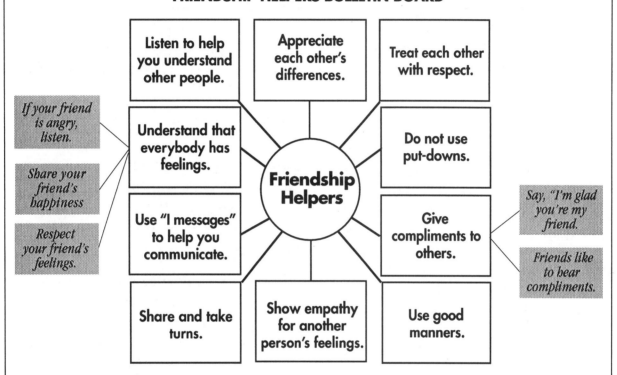

Re-create this "Friendship Helpers" diagram on a bulletin board. Review the behaviors and explain that each one that they have learned helps them to get along with others, as they already know. Pair up students and ask them to make a list of words or phrases about how one of the "friendship helpers" on the diagram might be used between friends to bring them closer together. For example, for "Appreciate each other's differences,"

students might list: finding out where you lived before you came here, knowing your family's customs, noting a different personal characteristic a student admires. Ask students to choose two ideas from their list that they think could be very important in a friendship and write them on smaller pieces of construction paper. Place the smaller pieces around the diagram (see examples in italics) and review all the ideas the students chose.

Note: Some of the activities on the next page refer to the diagram shown above.

Friendship Helpers Role-Play

List several situations on the board in which friends interact—for example: playing a game, talking on the phone, walking to school. Pair up students and ask them to choose one of the situations and perform it in a role-play that incorporates at least one of the Friendship Helpers. (You can provide a list of the helpers to each pair.) After the role-play, the class guesses which Friendship Helpers promoted the friendship.

Buddies for the Day

Pair up students and say that you'd like the partners to be "buddies" for the day. Have the partners interview each other (about hobbies, interests, family, where born and raised, favorite place to visit, customs, etc.) and write a paper entitled "What I Didn't Know About My Buddy." Students can read their paper to the class. Pairs work together for the day, participate in games that involve partners and choose free-time activities to do together. Remind students that as they work and play together on this special day to keep in mind the prosocial rules for getting along together the class has chosen (see Lesson #2, page 23).

You'd Be a Good Friend Because...

Have students draw a name of another student and write a compliment (on the compliment coupons on page 46) about a good quality the student has that would be important in a friendship. "To: Maya, From: Leo. You are a good friend because you share things with others.") Students can refer to their "Compliments for You and Me" lists (page 45). Make sure the recipients thank the senders when the compliments are delivered.

Special-Friend Story Starter

Post a picture of two children interacting—or a child and an animal (friendly dragon or bear). Ask students to write a story about describing how the two met, what happened to them and how they became friends. Tell students they can include in their stories some ideas from the Friendship Helpers Bulletin Board about what is important in a friendship.

Wanted: A Friend

Bring in samples of classified ads or re-create one on the board so students understand the style. Tell students they are to write a classified ad that seeks a friend, describing the activities and personal qualities that would be most important to them. An ad might read, for example: "Looking for a Good Friend. Must like baseball cards and playing a musical instrument. Needs to treat me with respect and understand my feelings. Must like popcorn."

What I Could Offer My Friend

Refer to the Friendship Helpers diagram and explain that everybody performs these skills differently—for example, some people are especially good listeners, other people are always respectful. Ask students to write a few paragraphs about what they think are the special qualities they could contribute to a friendship.

Secret Friend

Tell students to write in their journal about someone in class they might like to have as a friend. Ask them to describe the qualities and the mutual interests they think they both have that could contribute to the friendship. Students can also write what they think are the reasons the friendship has not so far been formed.

CHAPTER 4

Using Community Circles

You have set prosocial expectations that guide students in interacting with peers. You have taught students skills and strategies that will enhance their ability to get along with others. The next step is to build into every day a structured opportunity for students to practice prosocial skills and to think and talk about appropriate ways to interact with others. That's what a Community Circle is all about.

Encouraging Group Sharing with Community Circles

Perhaps you already include a group time in the school day. You may call it by another name— class meeting, sharing time, discussion circle. Basically, it's a time when the class gets together to talk through issues that are important to the group. And what could be a more vital issue than learning how to get along with others?

The value of having a structured time for discussing the ins and outs and ups and downs of getting along is that it becomes a routine that both you and students can count on. If there's a fight on the playground, you can explore in the Community Circle why the fight occurred and how to prevent such fights in the future. Students know they can raise behavior-related questions or concerns in the Community Circle. It guarantees that, despite the many demands pressing on your day, you make time daily to teach and promote positive social skills.

Scheduling Your Community Circle

Plan for your Community Circle at the same time each day, so that students can look forward to it. There's no one right time, though there are special advantages to holding a circle first thing in the morning or at the very end of the day.

A morning Community Circle helps you start the day on a positive note. It's an opportunity to gauge individuals' feelings and the mood of the class as a whole. Students who are troubled by an incident that occurred on the way to school, for example, can get it out in the open, rather than stewing about it all day. (For more specifics, see the first sample script, page 69.)

An afternoon Community Circle helps you end the day in an upbeat way. You can review the day's events and celebrate individual acts of kindness and camaraderie among class members. (See the second sample script, page 70.)

There may be times when you'll want to convene a special Community Circle to deal immediately as a group with a problem that has just occurred, such as a fight during the lunch period. Chances are, everyone in the class will know about the incident. By reviewing the events and exploring better ways to respond next time, you get what really happened out in the open—stopping rumors that could lead to other problems—and you help the whole group learn appropriate ways to deal with conflict. (See the third sample script, page 70.)

Because your Community Circle is a daily activity, you don't need to carve out a lot of time for it—say ten minutes, enough time to have a meaningful discussion. When there is a serious problem to tackle, such as a fight between two students, you may need to allow extra time to work through the problem-solving process and to summarize for the group key messages about getting along.

Keep in mind that consistency is vital. By making time for your Community Circle every day, you demonstrate to students that helping them learn to get along with others is a priority for you. But if you hold your Community Circle only when it's "convenient," then you risk sending a very different message: that using prosocial skills is something that students need not do all the time, but only when it's convenient for them.

Tips on Presenting Community Circles

What does a Community Circle look like? It starts with the class sitting in a circle on the floor. Why in a circle? Students need to see one another as they share. Observing others encourages communication and helps children learn to pick up on the nuances of body language, which offer silent clues to how others think and feel. Position yourself on the floor or on a low stool, to make it clear to students that you are a member of the circle, too.

Props help many students feel more comfortable sharing, keep the discussion more orderly, and make it easier for shy children to get a turn to speak. Introduce a small, soft ball that can be tossed from one child to the next, to designate whose turn it is to share. Refer to page 81, "Community Circle Tools" for more ideas of useful props to gather.

It's also important to identify specific expectations for this sharing time and to explain the purpose of each rule. For example:

- Listen carefully to others without interrupting.
- Only one person speaks at a time.
- Keep your hands to yourself.
- Stay seated.
- No put-downs.

On page 75 you'll find ★ *Lesson #13: Setting Expectations for Getting Along in a Community Circle*. Repeat the lesson now and then, to remind students of the reasons for gathering as a group and of the behavior you expect to see in a Community Circle.

Community Circles in Action

Here are three examples of how actual classroom teachers have used the Community Circle to:

- set a positive tone while also gauging what's happening in students' lives that affects their ability to get along with others;
- celebrate individuals' prosocial accomplishments;
- work through a problem, such as a fight on the playground.

Review these scripts for examples of open-ended questions and techniques that encourage students to share, as well as for models of how to present a problem to the group and probe to find solutions that both parties will see as fair.

Using the Community Circle to Set a Positive Tone for the Day

Teacher: To start off our day today, I want to let you know what's happening in my world. You know I've had a cold, and today I woke up without a voice. I was feeling very sad because I wanted to teach you the new song today that's part of our play. I was telling this to Mrs. Schack and she offered to teach the song to you. Wasn't that nice of her to help me out? So she'll be coming in later to teach our new song, and I know you'll all show her your appreciation by being very polite and cooperative. And thanks to Mrs. Schack, now I feel so much better. So that's what's happening in my world. What's happening in yours? Crystal? (*Throws ball to girl.*)

Crystal: I played my violin in the concert last night.

Teacher: Wonderful! Did anyone else go to the concert?

Siri: (*After ball is passed to her*) I did. The music was nice.

Teacher: Thank you, I'm sure Crystal appreciates hearing that from you. Don't you, Crystal?

Crystal: Yes. Thanks, Siri.

Teacher: Please pass the ball to another person who can tell us about what's happening in his or her world today.

Vonetta: (*After ball is passed to her*) Tomorrow is my birthday.

Teacher: All right! That's exciting. Class, we'll all want to remember to wish Vonetta a happy birthday tomorrow! Let's hear from Jordan next. It looks like he's got something new in his world.

Jordan: Oh, yeah. My glasses. I went to the eye doctor and he said I couldn't see well.

Teacher: And you've got beautiful new glasses. They're cool. Class, it's nice to be able to share what's happening in our worlds with each other. It helps us to know each other better and helps us get along.

There are several important things this teacher accomplishes in the Community Circle. To start, she reinforces for students that this is a time when they can share problems—in her case, laryngitis. By telling the class about her discussion with her colleague and her colleague's willingness to help out by teaching the class the new song, she models for children how adults get along and help one another. She also communicates to the class her expectations for how they will behave when working with the other teacher. She guides a student in acknowledging another student's positive comment, and she states her expectation that the class will acknowledge a peer's birthday the next day. She makes a point of helping a student through what could be a trying day and a source of teasing—sporting a pair of glasses for the first time. She sets the tone by saying something positive about the glasses and encouraging the boy to view his appearance as "cool." Finally, she reminds students of a very important key to getting along: getting to know others well.

Using the Community Circle to Celebrate Prosocial Behavior

Teacher: I like to sit in the Community Circle at the end of the day so we can talk about how things are going, about communicating with each other, and having respect for each other, too. Speaking of being thoughtful of each other and doing nice things, who can tell me something that happened today that was really nice and that you'd like to share with us? Allison? *(Tosses a ball to girl to indicate she may speak.)*

Allison: Christa and Kristin played kickball with me.

Teacher: And how did that make you feel?

Allison: Good.

Teacher: Who else has something positive to share? Allison, please toss the ball to Doug.

Doug: I was playing handball with Amir, and even though I got out, he said, "Nice try."

Teacher: And how did Amir's words make you feel?

Doug: I didn't feel as bad about getting out. And I felt that next time I would try harder to do better.

Teacher: I like taking time at the end of the day for the Community Circle and hearing positive things that happened to you and that you did for others. It's a great way to wind up our day. Tomorrow we can look forward to finishing our masks that we started making today. I can't wait to see how your masks are going to turn out! They're looking great!

Notice that the teacher starts by reviewing for students the purpose of the Community Circle. She states clearly that they are together to focus on how they get along as individuals and as a group. She encourages children to share examples of kindnesses others have shown them, and in so doing, holds these acts up as models of behavior. She asks children to recall how they responded to their peers' positive actions, to help students recognize the connection between how they treat others and how they make others feel. She also lets the group know that she enjoys these times with them. (And as you know, a teacher's enthusiasm is contagious. If you enjoy something, your students are more likely to enjoy it, too.) Finally, she previews an activity the group will do tomorrow, giving everyone something to look forward to.

Using the Community Circle to Work Through a Problem

Teacher: I need everyone to help resolve a conflict we had on the playground during lunch. Natalie, I'm going to pass the ball to you and I'd like you to tell us your side of what happened. Okay? And then we'll hear from the other side.

Natalie: I was on the rings, and then Anton jumped on the rings and I was kicking him and telling him to get off. Then I walked away.

Teacher: Okay. Now pass the ball to Anton. Anton, tell us in your own words what happened.

Anton: I was jumping on the rings and she was kicking me.

Teacher: You both sound very calm now, but when you were on the playground, you were very upset with each other. Natalie, what is a better way you could have solved this conflict?

Natalie: I could have told Anton to please get off the rings and stand in line and wait his turn.

Teacher: Right. You could have asserted yourself. Anton, what could you do differently next time?

Anton: When she was kicking me, I could tell her to stop it.

Teacher: Yes, rather than kicking back, that would be a better thing to do. But think about what you did that caused Natalie to kick you—what would you do next time? Anybody want to give Anton an idea?

Student: He could wait until it's his turn to use the rings.

Teacher: Great. He could wait his turn. People, do you think what happened was all Natalie's fault? Was it all Anton's fault?

Student: It was both of their faults.

Teacher: When we respond to someone who's bothering us with angry words or actions—when we call names or hit or scream—we make a problem bigger. Natalie and Anton both contributed to this problem. And they both need to resolve it. Did you notice that when Natalie told her side, and Anton told his, both of their stories sounded the same? They saw the same things happening. They need a way to resolve the situation that they both can live with. Natalie, if next time you just said, "Anton, please move," and didn't kick him; Anton, if next time you didn't jump on the rings while Natalie was on them; could you live with that solution and not have that conflict again?

Natalie and Anton: Yes.

Teacher: This is good for all of us because these kinds of problems happen to all of us. Thank you for helping us with this problem.

This teacher is taking advantage of a teachable moment in the Community Circle. There has been a fight with an unsatisfactory ending, and the teacher enlists the help of the whole group to resolve the situation. Naturally, you wouldn't want to engage in this type of problem solving until you have taught students specific skills for responding to conflict (see Chapter 6) and established a format for group discussion. If the classroom environment is not caring, dealing with problem-solving in a group could be embarrassing for the students involved and make matters worse.

Notice that the teacher informs the group immediately of the reason for this Community Circle. He lets each side share what happened and involves the other members of the circle in resolving the problem. Throughout the discussion, he helps everyone see that how this pair of students responded—kicking, screaming—escalated the problem. He puts the responsibility on the disputants to come up with better ways with which they could have responded. He emphasizes the importance of finding solutions that both sides can live with. Finally, he makes the discussion relevant for everyone by reminding students that they all experience conflict and need to know appropriate ways to respond.

More Ideas for Community Sharing

On pages 79 and 80 you'll find a variety of discussion starters to help students explore a range of topics and feelings in your Community Circle. Skim the lists for ideas your students will benefit from discussing or that you know they'll respond to. Remember, however, that it's not only the discussion topic that matters. Your physical presence in the circle and your commitment to it are vital. By planning frequent Community Circles, you communicate to students that the time the group spends together in the Community Circle is important; that what you discuss there is valuable; that you place a priority on helping every student learn to get along with others.

Make Your Community Circle
a Feelings Circle

Promoting good mental health is one of my main priorities in teaching students to get along. Many of my third-graders come from homes where there is a lot of strife, and their feelings are all mixed up. They haven't learned to control strong emotions. They don't recognize that their actions can make others feel bad—or good.

I use the Community Circle to talk about feelings, and I often schedule it during the time when I teach health. I always start by reviewing the rules of our circle. One of the most important is confidentiality. I remind students that we don't share what is said in the circle outside of it. So far a student has never broken that confidence.

We talk about all kinds of feelings in our Community Circle. I ask students to think about a time when they were silly . . . sad . . . happy . . . scared . . . ashamed . . . angry. . . . We take turns sharing our stories, and in the process, the children begin to recognize that everyone has the same feelings as they do. It becomes easier to help students understand that if being teased or called a name makes them feel sad or ashamed, teasing others or using put-downs makes other students feel sad, too. Our discussions have helped students to show more respect for others' feelings and to empathize more.

On other days, I introduce typical "what if?" situations that students encounter: Someone pushes you in the lunch line—what do you do? I invite students to share different ways they might respond to this problem. As a group, we analyze which actions will make the situation worse, and which will help to resolve it.

My third-graders really look forward to the Community Circle, and they eagerly share. It's an important routine in our classroom. It brings us together and creates a sense of family. And the good feelings that develop in the circle radiate in other ways, such as through our "friendship chain." Any time they want, students can take a precut strip of paper, write a compliment about a classmate, then loop it into a link to add to a class chain. It's all voluntary, and it takes a while at the start of the year for the chain to grow. But the more comfortable students get in the Community Circle, and the more their understanding of feelings develops, the longer the chain of compliments gets. Community Circles—good feelings—getting along: They're linked!

Kristin Reilly, Daytons Bluff Elementary
St. Paul, Minnesota

SETTING EXPECTATIONS FOR GETTING ALONG IN A COMMUNITY CIRCLE

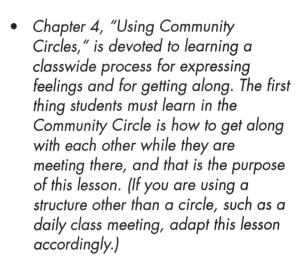

> *This is a good place to get to know each other.*

- *Chapter 4, "Using Community Circles," is devoted to learning a classwide process for expressing feelings and for getting along. The first thing students must learn in the Community Circle is how to get along with each other while they are meeting there, and that is the purpose of this lesson. (If you are using a structure other than a circle, such as a daily class meeting, adapt this lesson accordingly.)*

- *"Great Ideas: Community Circle Discussion Starters," page 79, provides a variety of ideas to facilitate interaction and expression of feelings.*

- *"Great Ideas: Community Circle Tools," page 81, describes items that are useful in the group process.*

PRIMARY OUTCOME

Students will be able to demonstrate the behavior necessary for getting along together in a Community Circle.

MATERIALS NEEDED

Anticipatory Set: Inflatable "world" ball

Follow-Up Activity #1: Shoeboxes

Follow-Up Activity #2: "I'd Like You to Know Me Better" reproducible, page 77

ANTICIPATORY SET

Seat students in a circle and hold up a "world" ball. Say, "This ball represents the world. All of the countries in the world make up a world community. People in the countries often meet with each other so that there is better understanding in the world. This happens in smaller communities too—our cities, our towns and even our neighborhoods. People meet and talk about how they could make their community better. They solve problems. In our classroom, we are going to do the same thing. Our classroom community is going to meet every day in a Community Circle."

INSTRUCTION

1. "What's good about sitting in a circle: We can see each other's faces, we can hear each other, there's no beginning, no end, everybody's equal. In our Community Circle we're going to learn and practice the skills that help us get along with each other (listening, manners, empathy, etc.). We'll talk about feelings and problems, celebrate things, and get to know ourselves and each other better."

2. "You all know that we have rules for getting along together in our classroom. We will need some special rules for our Community Circle, too":

   - "We'll take turns so that everybody will have a chance to participate. If you don't feel like participating, you can pass and skip your turn." Have students practice taking turns by passing the ball around the circle.

- "Only one person may speak at a time and the person speaking must be brief."

3. "Now we are each going to talk about something new or exciting that has happened lately in our lives. We will pass the ball around and only the person holding the ball may speak. If you don't feel like participating this time, you may pass the ball to the next person. I am holding the ball now, so I will begin by telling you. . ." Have students pass the ball around the circle as they each take a turn speaking.

4. "For the first week, we are going to meet after lunch (in the morning, at the end of the day) in this Community Circle to talk about getting along. Then we'll decide if the circle is helping us, and if after lunch each day is the best time to meet. We can also have an "extra" Community Circle meeting if we can't wait for the regular meeting to talk about something, such as a fight or another problem that we would like to take care of right away."

APPLICATION

Begin with an activity that is simple and focuses on allowing students to practice interacting.

Primary: "To practice sharing in our circle, we are going to all get a chance to tell each other what our favorite food is. This time, when the speaker is finished he or she will toss the ball to another person

anywhere in the circle. Remember, one person speaks at a time and the rest of us listen and look at the person who is talking, hands in lap. I have the ball so I will begin. My favorite food is. . . ."

Intermediate: Toss the ball (as in the directions for primary) and call on students to finish the sentence, "I think a Community Circle will help us. . ."

CLOSURE

Call on students to review the reasons for having a Community Circle and the rules for getting along together. ■

Follow-Up Activity

Activity #1: Ask students to bring a few things from home that represent them—a hat, a memento, part of a collection, photographs. The items must fit into a shoebox. Give each student an empty shoe box to decorate with construction paper and drawings, and fill with the items. Use the Community Circle to have students tell about themselves by describing the shoebox and its contents.

Activity #2: Give each student a copy of the "I'd Like You to Know Me Better" reproducible and have them draw a self-portrait and complete the sentence starters at the bottom of the page. Hang the portraits around the classroom and call on volunteers to read all students' answers to question #2.

Home Study Activity

Choose a topic from the "Community Circle Discussion Starters" on page 79. Ask students to complete the starter by writing a story at home. Discuss the stories the next day in the Community Circle.

Name _____

I'd Like You to Know Me Better

1. Draw a self-portrait.

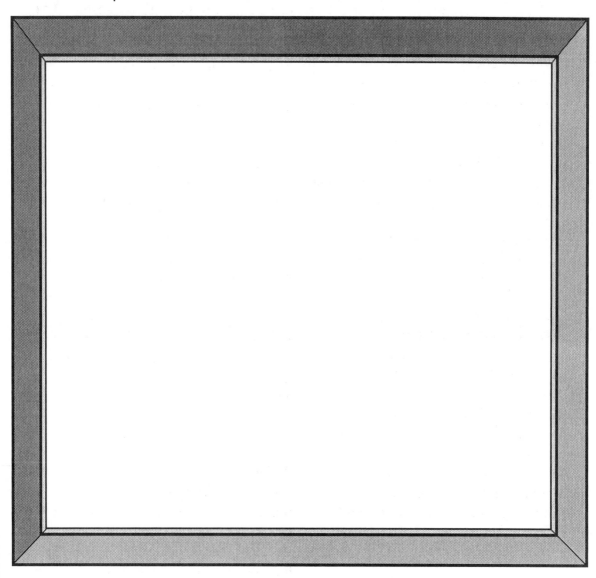

2. Complete the following:

- What I like best about myself is: _____

   _____

- What makes me unique is: _____

   _____

- I am special because: _____

   _____

Community Circle
Discussion Starters

Use the following discussion starters to encourage
communication in a Community Circle.

- I really get angry when. . .

- I am happy when. . .

- The funniest thing I ever saw was. . .

- If I saw a friend calling someone a name. . .

- The best time I had with my family was. . .

- My friend and I. . .

- When I grow up. . .

- If I could run the family. . .

- If I could run the classroom. . .

- I care about people who. . .

- When someone pushes me around I. . .

- I feel left out when. . .

- How I feel today is. . .

- One thing that happened in the last 24 hours that made me feel great is. . .

- I am proud of. . .

- One thing I am very good at is. . .

- I wish. . .

- A nice thing I did once for someone was. . .

- A nice thing someone did once for me was. . .

- My wish for today is. . .

- The scariest thing that ever happened to me was. . .

- My favorite place to visit is. . .

- The holiday I like best is. . .

- My favorite game is. . .

- After school I like to. . .

- The best gift I ever got was. . .

- My favorite TV show is. . .

- A nice thing that happened to me today is. . .

- When I'm alone I like to. . .

- My favorite color is. . .

- Being a friend means. . .

- I am proud of. . .

- Today I wish. . .

- Today I want. . .

- Today I will. . .

- One thing I look forward to is. . .

- My most special possession is. . .

- What I like best about my class is. . .

- A special memory I have is. . .

- My favorite thing to do with friends is. . .

- One nice thing I like to do with my family is. . .

- The most difficult thing I ever did was. . .

- One thing I would like to change about myself is. . .

- If I needed a safe place to go to think or to be alone, I would go. . .

- One change I have made this year that I feel proud of is. . .

- Something I lost that was important or special to me was. . .

- It is the beginning of a new year. What can each of you do to help make our classroom or school a safer place?

- You and your friends stopped by a snack place after school. You ordered juice but were served a soda. What will you do about it?

- What is one thing you dislike doing most? Why? What can you do about it?

- What is one thing you would like to do but need help from someone else to do it?

- Did you ever feel that you did not like someone when you first met him or her? Why? Did you change your mind? If you did, why did you?

- Do you like spending time alone or would you rather be with friends? Why?

- What do you look for in a friend? Do you choose a friend because of looks? Brains? Kindness or loyalty? Fun? Other reasons?

Add some of your own "starters":

-

-

-

-

-

-

-

-

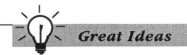

Community Circle Tools

*Use the following tools to facilitate the process
of conducting a Community Circle.*

Timer

A timer can help to signal the start of the Community Circle meeting and the end, especially for the students who become actively involved and have difficulty moving to the next activity.

Soft Ball (or other prop)

Make taking turns easier by using a prop such as a soft ball that can be passed from student to student. (Other ideas for props are: inflatable ball, stuffed animal, magic wand.) The ball encourages shy students to share and helps limit speaking time for students with a tendency to continue without stopping. You can also use the ball as a "check-in" activity to ascertain the emotional and physical state of students at the beginning of the day.

Pass the ball around the circle and tell students that only the person holding the ball is allowed to speak and share thoughts, concerns and feelings. The other students are to be quiet listeners. If a student takes too long to speak, remind the student of the rule to be brief, gently take the ball away, thank the student, and give the ball to someone else.

Puppets

Puppets can introduce a new activity, idea or concept. Puppets are excellent for leading group discussions, helping students with problem solving, encouraging shy students, and reminding students of Community Circle expectations for getting along together.

Students feel safer telling a story using a puppet because it feels more "anonymous." Students can use puppets to create open-ended stories and ask for ideas from the rest of the group. This creates a support system and provides additional options for solving conflicts.

Puppets can be used as a tool for role-playing. They provide the make-believe element students need for using their imagination creatively and allowing them to develop options rather than feel limitations.

Different puppets can be utilized as experts on various subjects:

- The Wizard: decision-making expert
- The Good Witch: problem-solving and conflict-resolution expert
- Honeybear: the storyteller
- Turtle or Snail: encouragement expert
- Wishing Bear: dream-maker
- Ostrich: risk-taker

Once students realize what each puppet is used for, they know when that puppet appears what they will be learning or discussing. They ask which puppet will they be having fun with that day. Older students like puppets as much as do younger students. Older students can write a script and put on shows for younger ones.

Mailbox

Students need an opportunity to communicate in a nonthreatening way. One method is to use a mailbox made from a shoe box with an opening on top. Long before some students feel safe sharing in a group, they will drop a note in the mailbox to express their thoughts, concerns and feelings. Designate a specific time for students to "mail" their notes so the activity will not become a distraction during work time. When using a mailbox, check it regularly, and, without using students' names, bring up their issues in the Community Circle.

CHAPTER 5

Using Cooperative Teams

Used consistently, the Community Circle is a powerful and enjoyable way of communicating to students the value of positive interactions with peers. To involve students in practicing prosocial skills in a more independent setting, you need to encourage small-group interaction. If you're using cooperative-group instruction in your classroom, you have ready-made teams for promoting social skills while developing subject-matter skills and knowledge. For teachers who have not yet adopted this effective instructional technique, you'll discover compelling reasons to start today. Cooperative teams show students in a very direct way why each person benefits when team members get along.

a role in the team, everyone feels needed and important. Because the team members are responsible for each other, every member has a stake in ensuring that every other member succeeds.

These characteristics of cooperative learning that make it such a useful technique for helping students learn subject-area content also make it effective in helping children learn prosocial skills—in helping them master the dynamics of group interaction. And as students become more proficient in working together as a team, they get more out of cooperative-learning activities. Using cooperative teams to promote prosocial skills is a win-win proposition, socially and academically.

Building Cohesiveness Through Cooperative Teams

Research has established the effectiveness of cooperative learning, when properly applied, as an instructional technique. Placing students of mixed ability in small teams enables children to learn from one another. With the variance of abilities and learning styles in our classrooms, working with others helps to reinforce skills and concepts for all students. Because everyone has

Structuring Successful Cooperative Teams

If you have never used cooperative teams in your class—or if you've shied away from doing so because of colleagues' complaints about students talking and acting out during group activities—these guidelines will help you ensure that your cooperative teams are truly cooperative. How you structure your cooperative teams has a very big impact on the overall success of those teams.

- **Limit teams to four to six students.**
  Research indicates this is the best size for
  cooperative activities. One student can too
  easily take over in a pairing; with three
  students, two often gang up on the third.
  Larger teams of seven or more are too big to
  ensure the full participation of every student.
  Teams of four to six students have more
  opportunities to get to know one another, and
  to practice those skills that enable them to get
  along.

- **Create teams that are diverse.** The best
  teams represent a mix of skills and
  strengths—students who can learn from one
  another as they learn to get along. You want
  some students who are leaders, some who are
  organizers, some who are more assertive,
  some who are more able academically, some
  who will benefit from working alongside all of
  these peers. You also want teams that are
  diverse in race, ethnicity, and gender, to
  encourage students to get to know classmates
  they might not otherwise spend time with.

  As you form your teams, don't make the
  mistake of thinking that each team will be
  more compatible if you put all of the shy
  children together or all of the more aggressive
  students, all of the smarter students, or all
  boys or all girls together. That shy group will
  flounder without a natural leader among its
  members; that aggressive group may get
  hopelessly sidetracked by arguments without
  a natural peacemaker in it. Those more-able
  learners may already be grouped together
  daily for reading or math. By grouping them
  for cooperative activities at other times, you
  deny them and their less academically skilled
  peers an opportunity to get to know each
  other better. And boys and girls need to learn
  to work together. Variety lends strength to
  cooperative teams.

- **Keep your teams together for at least one
  quarter of the year.** You want to help
  students not only learn to cooperate as a
  team, but to perfect those skills. It takes time
  to get to know one another—including
  individuals' strengths and weaknesses—to
  negotiate differences, to build trust. Once a
  team has worked through that process, give
  the members time to enjoy the fruits of their
  efforts, to recognize the benefits of being able
  to work as a team. It is important to vary the
  composition of your teams during the year, so
  that students get a chance to interact with a
  variety of peers. Just don't be *too* hasty to
  change those teams before students have
  gotten the most from them. But *do* change
  them at some point; change will create an
  energized climate. For noncooperative
  learning tasks, create other groups—variety
  keeps interest high.

- **Start teams with activities that help them
  get to know their fellow members.** Even if
  you do all of the above, your cooperative
  teams will easily fail if you don't take the time
  to help teammates get to know each other's
  likes, dislikes, interests, and so on. This is
  certainly true at the beginning of the year,
  when you are forming teams for the first time,
  but it's also true in the winter or in the spring,
  when you're changing teams again. Just
  because students are together in the same
  classroom doesn't mean they know every
  classmate well. They know those students
  who are their closest friends. There may be
  many compatible interests among other
  classmates that are yet to be discovered.

- **Help members create a team identity.**
  Why does every sports team name itself and
  have a logo? A team identity creates a sense of
  union, of group cohesiveness. You want to
  encourage that same feeling of uniqueness
  and team loyalty within your cooperative
  teams. Take time to let each team create an
  identity for itself.

Keeping Cooperative Teams on Track and on Task

If there is one word that you'll hear again and again in relation to helping students learn to get along, it's *expectations*. You need to set expectations for how students will interact with one another in the classroom, outside the classroom, in the Community Circle, and *in cooperative teams*. When you state your behavioral expectations, students know what is acceptable behavior toward peers and what is not.

Stating your expectations for cooperative-group activities is especially important because you cannot be with five or six teams at once. Teams need to function more or less independently: to know the task at hand, to know each member's role, and then to proceed.

Think about the rules that will encourage students to work well together and avoid confrontations; for example:

- Contribute to your team.
- Only one person speaks at a time.
- Give everyone a chance to speak.
- Listen carefully to others.
- Use an "inside" (quiet) voice.
- No put-downs.

Use ★ *Lesson #14: Setting Expectations for Getting Along in Cooperative Teams*, on page 89, to teach students the prosocial behaviors necessary for working together in a cooperative team. Repeat this lesson each time you form new cooperative teams, or whenever students need to be reminded of your prosocial expectations for small-group interaction.

Backing Up Your Rules with Consequences

When you teach your behavior expectations for working in cooperative teams, at the same time, inform students of the consequences for inappropriate behavior. Check to be sure students understand them.

Remember that the most effective consequences relate to the activity at hand. Start with a warning for a first offense, to give students a chance to correct their behavior. A consequence for a second offense might involve removing the student from the team for a while. A more serious consequence for repeated misbehavior might be to make the student responsible for completing the task on his or her own. Use your judgment based on your knowledge of your students, but be sure that your consequences would not humiliate or physically or emotionally harm a student.

Assigning Special Roles

By definition, a cooperative team is a group of students who each have a special job to carry out in order for the team to complete its task. Assigning each team member a special role also helps to keep the team on task.

Typical jobs, which may vary depending on the task, are *organizer* (gathers materials or resources the team needs); *leader* (makes sure the team stays on task); *questioner* (checks how the team is thinking and makes sure all ideas are explored); *recorder* (writes down the team's ideas); *artist* (creates pictures or illustrates ideas); *timekeeper* (makes sure the team finishes within allotted the time); and *reporter* (presents team's ideas to the rest of the class).

By giving each member a role, you also ensure greater equality within the team. Every member makes a contribution, so every member feels like an important part of the team. By rotating the roles among team members, so that individuals don't assume the same job every time, you lessen the tendency of some students to take over. By defining clear roles for team members, you make it easier for students to work together and get along.

Use ★ *Lesson #15: Understanding the Importance of Team Roles*, on page 95, to introduce students to these roles and help them understand how taking special roles helps the team perform its work better.

Reinforcing and Redirecting Cooperative Teams

Once your teams are off and running, does that mean you can use this time for grading or catching up on other paperwork? After all, students know your expectations. But are you confident that every student in every team will follow those rules? Naturally, we know that only in a dream class would that be the case. Remember, it's going to take patience and practice to help students learn to get along in appropriate ways. Students need your guidance—your attention—to help them meet your prosocial expectations.

Circulate among the teams as they work. You'll be available to answer questions about the task and to monitor individuals' behavior. Just your physical proximity will often stop a student who is starting to act out or to take control of the group. Saying a student's or a pair's name is another way to get wandering minds (or hands or feet) refocused: "Maria and Angelina, are you thinking about this problem with your team?" Or commend students who *are* listening to their peers or clearly concentrating on their assigned tasks. Watch for examples of cooperation or thoughtfulness to applaud, such as when Alexia reminds the team that John, a quiet boy, hasn't had a chance to speak yet. Everyone will get the

message when they see the kinds of behaviors you single out for praise.

Listen, also, for arguments or fights which are brewing that require you to intervene. For example, from across the room, you see Amy and Jennifer pulling a paper back and forth between them. Don't wait. Move quietly (so you don't distract teams that are on task) and quickly (so you don't let the problem escalate) to that team. Find out what the problem is: Amy didn't want to be the recorder, so Jennifer took the job; now Amy wants to record the team's ideas. Address your attention to Amy. In a firm but calm voice, state that her behavior is unacceptable. Remind her of your expectations for group work: She must do her assigned job. Tell her that she has a choice to work cooperatively with her team or to choose the consequences. Express your confidence in her ability to work with Jennifer and her other teammates, and praise Amy as she gets refocused.

A Strategy That Really Works

Don't shy away from using cooperative teams in your classroom. True, they require more management expertise than having students sitting in rows, working alone. But from our experience in classrooms, observing the strategies that have the most potential to develop prosocial skills, placing students in cooperative teams is number one. It's the best way to show students why getting along with others is in their interest; that it makes doing a task easier and more enjoyable.

Working with others on a team is essential in many jobs. Help your students get ready for more successful futures by giving them the means and the opportunity to learn to share ideas, pool resources, and work productively as a member of a cooperative team.

Group Work Helps Students
Get to Know Each Other

As a middle-school science teacher, I'm working with students who are at an age when their peers are very important to them. Early adolescents are very concerned about fitting in, about being a member of the group. One of the biggest social problems I see is cliques. A group of kids travels together, and they exclude other students, who feel hurt. Those kinds of problems between students can spill over into the classroom.

There is no one solution when students have problems getting along. As a teacher, you have to take several steps. I set, and enforce, prosocial expectations for how students will interact in my classroom. I expect them to treat each other with respect. I am also fair but *consistent* in backing up my rules with consequences. Students have to know that you mean business.

I also use cooperative grouping in my classroom; in fact, more than ever before. It's not only an effective instructional technique, it's a great way to help students get to know other students they don't pal around with.

As a former school football coach, I know the value of helping students develop teamwork skills. I look for ways to motivate students to work together in teams, such as by giving them time to get to know their team members and develop a team identity.

After 28 years in the classroom, I've learned that you have to *teach* students skills like teamwork and cooperation. Giving students frequent opportunities to work in small groups is a natural way to do it.

John Sekela, Laurel Valley Middle School
New Florence, Pennsylvania

Lesson #14

SETTING EXPECTATIONS FOR GETTING ALONG IN COOPERATIVE TEAMS

My group knows how to get along together.

PRIMARY OUTCOME

Students will be able to demonstrate the specific rules necessary for working in Cooperative Teams.

MATERIALS NEEDED

Anticipatory Set: Colored paper cut into shapes

Application: "Cooperative Teams Checklist: Following the Rules for Getting Along" reproducible, page 91

Follow-Up Activity: "Cooperating, Getting Along" reproducible, page 92

ANTICIPATORY SET

Using a different color for each Cooperative Team, cut paper into various shapes—for example, red paper cut into circles, yellow paper cut into strips. Tape the pieces under the students' desks. Tell students, "At the count of three, look under your desks and remove the paper pieces. Find the people who have the same color and shape, and sit together quietly." When each group has been formed, say, "Congratulations. You have just formed special groups that we are going to call Cooperative Teams."

INSTRUCTION

1. "What is the purpose of a Cooperative Team? The purpose is to work together while we're learning.

Instead of working separately, we'll put our heads together and come up with bigger and better ideas. We can cooperate in a team while we're learning math, or studying spelling words, or while we're reading. Doing these things together shows us that we can get along with each other while we are working, not just while we are having fun.

2. "To help work in Cooperative Teams, we are going to learn how to get along while we're in a team."

- First review the prosocial expectations for the class that you determined and taught previously (see lessons for Chapter 2) by asking students to remind you what the rules are. Tell students that these rules are in effect at all times and therefore will also apply when they are working in Cooperative Teams.

- Explain that in addition to the rules for getting along together for the classroom, there are some special rules for when students are working in groups. List the following rules on the board (note: some may be the same as your classroom rules):

  – Contribute to your team.

  – One person speaks at a time, using an "inside" (quiet) voice.

- Give everyone a chance to speak.
- Listen carefully to others.
- Do not use put-downs.

4. Ask students to role-play the behaviors or describe what the rules mean.

APPLICATION

The focus of this activity is on the behavior in the team, not on the task.

Give each student a copy of the "Cooperative Teams Checklist: Following the Rules for Getting Along" and review it with students. Select a topic from "Community Circle Discussion Starters" on page 79 and ask students to discuss it in their teams. Then ask them to mark their checklists and discuss if, during the activity, the team members behaved according to the rules for getting along.

CLOSURE

"Why is it important that we have rules for getting along together in Cooperative Teams?" Elicit responses, then say, "When you know how to get along in our Cooperative Teams, two things will happen: You will be more successful with your work because you are getting along and helping each other, and you will be having more fun while you are learning." ■

Follow-Up Activity

Primary: Distribute a copy of the "Cooperating, Getting Along" song to each student. Have the Cooperative Teams discuss the meaning of the lyrics. Then teach the song.

Intermediate: Ask the teams to observe the rules for getting along in their group while they perform the following activity: 1) As a team, discuss, define and write down the meaning of the word "cooperation." 2) Look up the word in a dictionary. 3) Decide if the group's definition needs to be changed. 4) Make needed changes. After the groups have finished, call on each team to evaluate their efforts at following the rules for getting along in the group.

Home Study Activity

Primary: Ask students to cut out and bring to school pictures in magazines or newspapers of groups working together. Have the teams make a collage of the pictures and post the artwork around the classroom.

Intermediate: Ask students to write about a team or group they have been a part of outside of school, such as a scout troop, sports team, or church group. Ask them to describe the purpose of the group, what the group does, its rules, and the group roles (rank, officers, position on a team, committee member designations).

Team Name _____

COOPERATIVE TEAMS CHECKLIST

Following the Rules for Getting Along

Put a check mark in the box if everyone in your Cooperative Team followed the rules for getting along while you were learning.

☐   Contribute to your team.

☐   One person speaks at a time.

☐   The speaker uses an "inside" (quiet) voice.

☐   Give everyone a chance to speak.

☐   Listen carefully to others.

☐   Do not use put-downs.

Team Name _____

COOPERATIVE TEAMS CHECKLIST

Following the Rules for Getting Along

Put a check mark in the box if everyone in your Cooperative Team followed the rules for getting along while you were learning.

☐   Contribute to your team.

☐   One person speaks at a time.

☐   The speaker uses an "inside" (quiet) voice.

☐   Give everyone a chance to speak.

☐   Listen carefully to others.

☐   Do not use put-downs.

COOPERATING,

GETTING ALONG

Music and Lyrics
by Gail Schack

Shake a hand it's ea-sy to do. It will help solve problems for you.

Talk it out say what is true. That will solve prob-lems

for me and you. Lis-ten carefully right from the start.

Care for each oth-er with all your heart.

©1995 Gail Schack

Lee Canter & Associates PD4109

Using Cooperative Teams

UNDERSTANDING THE IMPORTANCE OF TEAM ROLES

We'll each do our part.

PRIMARY OUTCOME

Students will be able to perform the duties of the various roles assigned for working in Cooperative Teams.

MATERIALS NEEDED

Follow-Up Activity: "Cooperative Teams Word Puzzle" reproducible, page 97; "Let's Celebrate Teamwork" reproducible, page 98

ANTICIPATORY SET

List the following Cooperative Team roles on the board: Leader, Recorder, Reporter, Artist, Timekeeper. (Note: You may want to add other roles.)

INSTRUCTION

1. "As you know, you will be spending a lot of time in your Cooperative Teams this year, so it is important to take the time to discuss what responsibilities each of you will have in your team."

2. "If a team is going to be successful, the members have to depend on each other to do their jobs—for example, the players in a baseball team. Can you think of some other teams where each person has a special role or responsibility?" (Examples: actors in a TV show, construction workers building a house, the people who design, build and ride in a space shuttle)

3. Introduce the individual roles you listed on the board and tell students that these are examples of responsibilities that can be assigned to team members. Explain that depending on the activity the team will be doing, there may be other roles. Elicit from students why they think each of the roles listed might be needed in a team—for example:

   - The Leader helps everyone in the team work together and stay on task.

   - The Recorder writes down important points that the team needs to remember.

   - The Reporter speaks for the group, referring to the notes, if needed, and presents ideas to other teams or to the rest of the class.

   - The Artist makes drawings or other creative items needed for an activity.

   - The Timekeeper keeps track of the time given by the teacher to complete an activity and helps the team stay on task and finish on time.

4. "What could happen to a baseball game if each member on the team didn't have a role? What could happen to. . . (refer to the projects

you discussed in Step #2—examples: TV show, house, space shuttle). What could happen to your work in your Cooperative Team? Which way is better for a team: If people have roles with certain responsibilities, or if there are no roles? Why?"

5. Tell students that at the beginning of each week (two weeks, etc.) they will be assigned a different role so that everybody has an opportunity to carry out different responsibilities for their team.

APPLICATION

The focus of this activity is on performing roles in the team, not on the task.

Ask students to form their groups, then assign roles to each student. Tell the teams that they are each going to think of a name for their team, then design a logo—a design composed of pictures and/or words that represents their team. Tell them to practice their roles while conducting the activities. The Leader manages the discussion, the Recorder takes notes, the Timekeeper keeps the group on task, the Artist draws the logo and the Reporter presents the finished work to the class.

CLOSURE

Call on students to answer the question, "What did you learn about your role while you were working in your Cooperative Team?" Then say, "When people on a team know what their roles are and what they have to do, the team works together better. When the team members carry out their roles as they are

supposed to, it shows they care about the success of the team and about the people in it." ■

Follow-Up Activity

Primary: Have students decorate role labels that you will laminate. Students keep the role labels in front of them as they work in the group so they will remember what they are supposed to do.

Intermediate: Give each student a copy of the "Cooperative Teams Word Puzzle" reproducible. Ask them to complete it, then look up and define any words they don't understand. Discuss the meaning of the words as they might apply to Cooperative Teams.

Additional Activity: Encourage students to recognize and celebrate positive events that take place in their Cooperative Teams during the week by giving each group a copy of the "Let's Celebrate Teamwork" reproducible. For each day, the group's Recorder writes down the positive things that happened. At the end of each day, collect the data and recognize each group in the Community Circle meeting for supporting and caring about its members.

Home Study Activity

Ask students to write about a role they have at home and what they believe their responsibilities are regarding the role. (Note: They may have more than one role—for example: son, brother, grandson, pet feeder, dishwasher.) Ask them to determine how their role contributes to the family "team." Primary students can draw a picture of them performing their role.

Cooperative Teams
Word Puzzle

D	B	E	H	A	V	I	O	R	A	L	R	Y
A	C	C	O	U	N	T	A	B	L	E	F	C
G	T	O	S	U	C	C	E	S	S	A	H	Z
R	R	E	O	U	B	E	Y	P	B	D	G	A
E	U	W	A	P	N	X	O	R	T	E	A	M
E	S	D	E	P	E	N	D	E	T	R	E	T
M	T	O	F	D	S	R	T	I	O	O	A	L
E	R	U	N	I	T	Y	A	I	E	Q	U	O
N	O	O	B	G	H	I	T	T	Y	G	M	Y
T	L	L	C	C	A	Z	L	X	I	R	O	A
R	E	S	P	E	C	T	P	S	L	O	R	L
C	S	E	Q	U	A	L	I	T	Y	U	N	T
A	O	P	L	E	Q	D	E	R	R	P	W	Y

FIND THESE WORDS:

LOYALTY	LEADER	BEHAVIOR	ACCOUNTABLE
DEPEND	COOPERATION	RESPONSIBLE	TEAM
TRUST	AGREEMENT	GROUP	ROLES
EQUALITY	SUCCESS	UNITY	RESPECT

Let's Celebrate Teamwork!

Each day, write down the positive things that happened in your team.

Monday: _____

_____

_____

_____

Tuesday: _____

_____

_____

_____

Wednesday: _____

_____

_____

_____

Thursday: _____

_____

_____

_____

Friday: _____

_____

_____

_____

CHAPTER 6

Teaching Skills for Responding to Conflict

So far we have been focusing on strategies that promote positive interactions among students and prevent conflict from occurring. But those skills only prepare students for half the challenge of learning how to get along with others. Just as important, students must learn how to respond to conflict in appropriate ways.

We've said it before, but it's worth repeating: Conflict is an inevitable part of life, because anger and frustration are normal, human emotions. Naturally, we can decrease the incidence of anger in our classrooms. Research indicates that a key reason why students get angry is stress. The more we reduce the level of stress in the classroom—especially the interpersonal stress that causes students and students or teachers and students to lock horns—the less anger there'll be. Such strategies as Community Circles and cooperative teams create a supportive network that promotes understanding and alleviates stress.

However, try as we may, we cannot protect students from all conflict; nor in truth, do we necessarily want to. Learning how to deal with conflict—how to negotiate, when to compromise, when to let the other person have his or her own way—is another essential life skill. We can learn a great deal about ourselves and others through experiences that involve peaceful resolutions of conflict.

Promoting Peaceful Solutions

Perhaps *peaceful* is the operative word. You know that too many conflicts among students end in physical confrontations or in verbal fist fights. Too many students don't know how to manage anger. Too many students don't know how respond to disagreements in ways that can become learning experiences for both parties.

Helping students learn appropriate ways to respond to conflict is the goal of this chapter. Beginning on page 105, you'll find lessons for teaching a range of applicable skills:

- how conflict escalates and how to know when to stop;
- how to respond assertively in conflict situations;
- how to manage anger by learning to stop and think before acting;
- how to use negotiating skills to resolve conflicts in mutually agreeable ways so that both parties "win."

Like prosocial skills, these are *teachable* skills. Many students don't know how to deal with conflict in appropriate ways because no one has showed them how.

But make no mistake, these students do have a strategy for handling conflict: aggression. They've learned it from their role models on television, in the neighborhood, or at home. They hit, punch, call names, isolate others because they've seen those techniques used and they've seen them work—at the expense of someone else's dignity or physical well-being, of course.

You have to counteract those lessons with others, and you'll find plenty of help and ideas in this chapter. With age-appropriate activities and many opportunities to reinforce these skills, you can replace those aggressive responses with more acceptable ones.

Teaching Students to Respond Assertively to Conflict

When faced with conflict, some people fight back with angry words or physical blows; some simply give up and let the other person win; and some can hold their ground without getting verbally or physically violent.

The first response is called an angry response. The second is a passive response. The third is an assertive response. You want to help students learn to respond assertively in conflict situations. To understand why the assertive response is the most effective, let's look more closely at each one.

The Angry Response

Chances are, you see this type of response from some students all the time. Someone jumps ahead of them in line, so they push the student out of the way. Someone grabs a ball they're playing with, so they grab the ball back. When students respond in this manner to a problem situation, they respond with unchecked anger. They yell, call names, punch, hit—the litany of behaviors is probably pretty familiar. Whatever the particular behavior, the key is that an angry response *escalates* the confrontation. It can easily cause a minor incident to blow up into a major fight.

Use ★*Lesson #16: Understanding the Escalation of Conflict*, page 105, to help students understand how a conflict can worsen and how they can stop a confrontation from getting out of control.

The Passive Response

For another group of students—those who tend to be "the victims" and the objects of bullying behavior—conflict renders them helpless. They may whine, cry, or respond with a weak-willed "leave me alone" or "don't do that." But if someone jumps ahead of them in line or takes the ball they're playing with, they pretty much feel powerless. A confrontation is likely to end quickly, because they just give up.

In some situations, such as when faced with an aggressor who is much stronger or who has a weapon, the passive response is the smart one. However, passive students always give in. The anger they feel goes inward, where that pent-up emotion works against their own physical and emotional well-being. Not expressing anger or hurt feelings can be just as damaging for these students as expressing it unchecked is for the angry ones.

The Assertive Response

Students who respond assertively to conflict know how to stand up for themselves in acceptable ways. If someone cuts ahead of them in line, they state clearly: "I was here first. Please go to the back of the line." They don't call names. They don't push the other person. But they will restate as many times as necessary what they want to see happen: the other person will go to the end of the line.

It's not easy for children (or adults) to respond consistently in an assertive way. It takes control to keep anger in check. Sometimes it takes "guts" to stand up for yourself. But what students learn as they use an assertive style is that it works! It's a strong response, but it doesn't challenge the other's person self-respect. It doesn't force the other person to "save face," as the angry response often does. Nor does it communicate that you can be pushed around, as the passive response does. An assertive response tells the other person what you want in a way that your message gets heard!

Help students learn to respond assertively to conflict by showing them what an assertive posture looks and sounds like. Teach ★*Lesson #17: Learning Assertiveness Skills*, page 109, and review those skills frequently.

Modeling the Assertive Response to Conflict

Responding to conflict with a calm voice and demeanor can be one of the most difficult behaviors for teachers to model consistently. When Peter acts out for the third time today, our blood pressure goes up. We've had it with Peter. All too easily we may respond with a red-faced, bellowing "What did I tell you, young man?" But when we do that, we send students the message that it's okay to react to conflict with a loud voice and angry words.

Teachers who treat students in an angry way create a classroom environment where students are hostile to one another. It's the old axiom at work: Actions speak louder than words. We can tell students to follow the "Golden Rule," but if we as teachers don't treat children, colleagues, or parents with respect, those hollow words will land on deaf ears.

Think about the three behavior styles for responding to conflict. Be honest with yourself about which one you tend to use most often, and work to model the most effective style, an assertive response. State clearly what you want, but in a way that maintains a student's dignity. Keep in mind that having a classroom discipline plan in place will help you stay in control when students act out.

Teaching Students to Manage Anger

Do you always know when you're angry? Chances are, you probably do. Most adults have learned to recognize the feelings that signal particular emotions, such as anger, frustration, love, joy, satisfaction. Children, on the other hand, are in various stages of emotional development. Some of your students will be farther along than others in learning to identify and understand their own emotions and those of others.

For students to be able to control their own anger, they need to recognize the physical signals that tell them they're feeling angry. Talk about these warning signs: feeling tense; feeling warm or hot as blood pressure rises; feeling an urge to punch, hit, or lash out; feeling like you could explode inside. Invite students to share other ways they know they are angry. Ask volunteers to recall times when they were angry and what caused them to be angry. Help students relate that not following your prosocial expectations—teasing, using put-downs, not sharing, not taking turns—can make others angry.

Use ★ *Lesson #18: Learning to "Stop, Think and Act,"* page 113, to help students learn what to do when they feel angry. You'll find that all students can benefit from this lesson, not just those with "short fuses."

Teaching Students Conflict-Resolution Skills

Helping students learn how to state their feelings without hurting the feelings of others and how to control their anger without lashing out at others are foundation skills. If students can't do the former, they won't have success in learning to work through their problems to find mutually agreeable solutions.

The concept of a "win-win" resolution can be difficult for students to understand. From movies and television, they are far more used to the idea of someone winning and someone losing. Students believe you negotiate to see who will win. Talk about what it means to reach an agreement that both sides can live with—that both sides can win. Help students understand that resolving a conflict involves thinking about what each person did, why it caused a problem, and what each could have done instead. It involves figuring out a plan of action that both sides feel is fair.

Finding win-win solutions is what diplomacy is all about. Nations often have trouble coming up with those settlements, so it's no wonder that children do, too. But you can help your students learn the art of negotiating fair resolutions to conflicts. ★ *Lesson #19: Learning Negotiating Skills*, page 119, will guide you. And imagine, if all people could learn negotiating skills at a young age, consider the potential for improved human relations in the future!

Teach Parents
These Techniques, Too

Having an emotionally disturbed student in my second-grade class taught me the value of knowing how to help students control anger. It also showed me that such techniques are doubly effective when parents use them, too.

When this boy got upset, he would get very aggressive and choke or hit other children. He needed to learn to channel his anger in appropriate ways. While I taught the whole class the Stop, Think and Act approach to managing anger, I spent extra helping him learn the steps. We went over them again and again, and in time, it made a difference. He learned to recognize when he was angry and to stop before he physically hurt another child.

I also shared the Stop, Think and Act technique with his mother. Now we were both using the same approach to helping him control his anger. That kind of consistency is vital for all children, but especially for emotionally disturbed students. His behavior at home improved, too.

Although this student had serious problems in getting along with other children, every student can benefit from learning the difference between effective and inappropriate responses to conflict and anger. Every student benefits from learning to interact positively with classmates—in learning how to pay compliments, for example. We have to be realistic about what children can learn at home about being part of a group. Kids are often the center of attention at home. They're not interacting with 20 other children. Getting-along skills are ones that need to be taught in school.

I've benefited, too, from learning to focus on the positive behaviors in my classroom. Before, I tended to concentrate on the negative—on how kids weren't getting along. I didn't consciously look for examples of students who were demonstrating kindness, consideration, cooperation, teamwork. Today I do, because the more of those behaviors that I can highlight and applaud, the more I'll see.

Dottie Hall, Pope Elementary
Jackson, Tennessee

Lesson #16

UNDERSTANDING THE ESCALATION OF CONFLICT

Stop conflicts before they get worse.

Lessons #1, 2 and 3 are closely connected and should be taught within a few days of each other.

PRIMARY OUTCOME

Students will be able to determine the point at which they believe it would be most effective to stop a conflict.

MATERIALS NEEDED

Application: "How Conflict Grows" reproducible, page 108

ANTICIPATORY SET

"I want to tell you a story about two friends at recess who were playing with a ball. Lisa was having such a good time playing that she threw the ball harder than she meant to and hit Shirelle on her leg. Shirelle started to cry and Lisa said, 'You're such a crybaby!' Shirelle became even more upset and said, 'You hit me on purpose! I don't want to play with you any more!' Lisa said angrily, 'I don't care! I don't like to play with crybabies anyway!' Lisa and Shirelle's fun ended with very bad feelings between them."

"Did these students get along together in the way we've been learning? Did Lisa use good manners and apologize for hitting Shirelle, and show empathy because she cried? Did Shirelle use an 'I message' to tell Lisa, 'I wish you'd be more careful when you throw the ball so I won't get hurt'?"

"Lisa and Shirelle had a conflict. Conflict in our classroom can happen when—like Lisa and Shirelle—you haven't followed the skills for getting along that you have learned, such as sharing, listening, good manners, and showing empathy. You are going to learn that you can stop and think about what to do when you have a conflict so that it won't get worse."

INSTRUCTION

1. "Let's talk about what conflict is. Many times you or I will disagree with another person—have a conflict. It's normal. We can't always agree with every single thing every person says or does. What kind of conflicts or disagreements do we see at home? In our community? In the world? What kind of conflicts happen in our classroom?" List the responses to each category on the board. "We can see that conflict can be as small as an argument or as big as a war.

2. "When you have a conflict or disagreement with someone, and you don't do what we've learned for getting along with each other, the conflict might get worse. Let's see what could happen if a conflict keeps growing." Re-create the "How Conflict Grows" reproducible by drawing it on the board. First describe the situation: Two students are playing with a ball.

Then, within each circle, list the steps of the escalating conflict. Exaggerate the conflict to dramatize the point: (center circle) Each student wants the ball; students argue and fight; more students join in; people everywhere join in; and so on until the fight spreads to other countries and eventually (in the outer circle) the whole world is fighting over the ball.

Example:

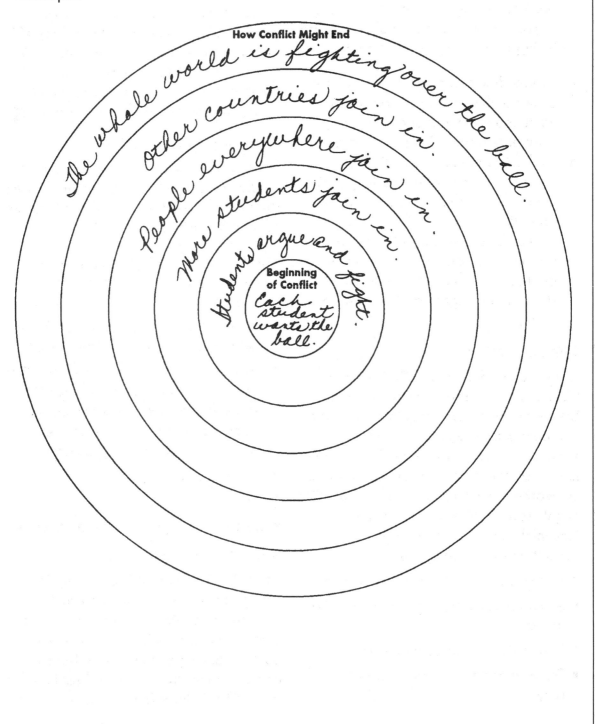

How Conflict Might End

The whole world is fighting over the ball.

Other countries join in.

People everywhere join in.

More students join in.

Students argue and fight.

Beginning of Conflict

Each student wants the ball.

3. "Of course, having a fight over a ball doesn't really mean that everybody in the world is going to start fighting. It just shows you that if a conflict isn't stopped, it can get much worse. An argument over a ball could end up with two friends who don't play with each other any more, or stop talking to each other. Or they might even start hitting and someone might get hurt."

4. "If you didn't want the conflict at the center of this drawing to get worse, what could have happened if you stopped it here?" Point to the outer circle. "It's too late, isn't it? Everybody in the world is already fighting." Work towards the center step by step repeating the question until you get to the center of the circle. "This is the best time to work things out—in the beginning—when people are first starting to disagree and are getting angry."

APPLICATION

Give each student a copy of the "How Conflict Grows" reproducible worksheet. List the following scenarios on the board and conduct a discussion about how each conflict might escalate. Ask students to choose one of the scenarios and list on the worksheet the steps of how the conflict might escalate. Ask them to identify when they think is the best time to stop the conflict and work things out.

- Two students want same seat on bus.

- A student is spreading rumors about a friend.

- Two students want to be first in line.

- Three students want the lead in the play.

CLOSURE

"We can expect disagreements to happen in our class, because we're all different— we think different things and we want different things. If we want to work out our disagreements because we respect each other, they won't get worse. When do you think is the best time to begin working out conflicts with other people?" Elicit response: the earlier the better. "In the next few days, you are going to be learning how to work things out at the beginning, before the conflict grows." ■

Follow-Up Activity

Primary: Have students interview the guidance counselor or the principal in the classroom about the kinds of conflicts that occur in the school.

Intermediate: Ask students to give examples, aloud or in writing, of the following:

- Conflicts that are serious—ones that if not stopped lead to disastrous results.

- Conflicts that are productive—ones that if handled well produce beneficial results. (For example: treaties between nations, contracts between workers and employers, teams playing a game.)

- Conflicts at home.

- Conflicts at school.

- Conflicts on TV programs or in literature.

Home Study Activity

Intermediate: Ask students to bring in newspaper articles about a conflict. Choose some articles to read aloud, and guide students to help you list the steps of each escalating conflict on the board, and when they think was the best time for the conflict to have been stopped.

Name _____

How Conflict Grows

1. Describe what was happening before the conflict started: _____

_____

2. Write in each circle what you think each stage might be in a conflict that is getting worse because nobody stops it.

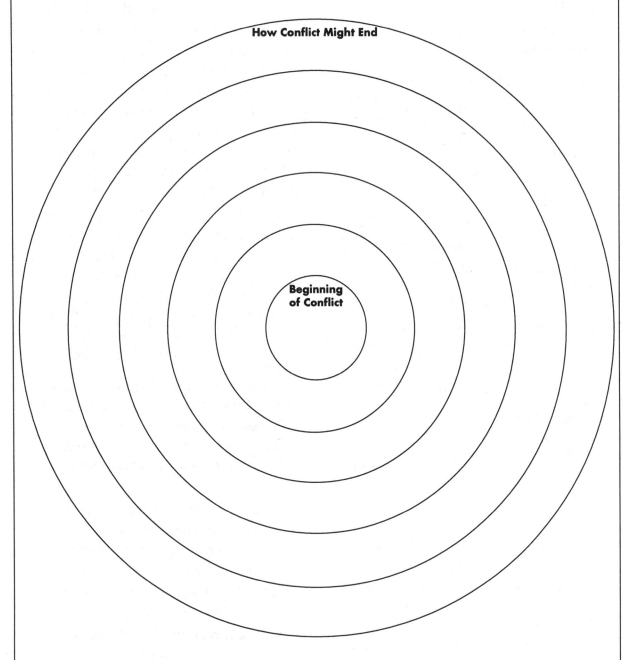

How Conflict Might End

Beginning of Conflict

3. Draw an arrow from here ● to the circle you think is the best time to stop the conflict.

LEARNING ASSERTIVENESS SKILLS

I can stand up for myself.

PRIMARY OUTCOME

Students will demonstrate the skills for behaving assertively in conflict situations.

MATERIALS NEEDED

Follow-Up Activity: "We Can Be Assertive" reproducible, page 111

Home Study Activity: "Being Assertive Word Puzzle," page 112

ANTICIPATORY SET

"Yesterday I dropped my lunch money." (For intermediate students say, "Yesterday I dropped a ten-dollar bill.") "Then I overheard that someone found some money. I thought it might be mine and I became really upset because I wasn't sure what to do about it. Today you are going to learn what you can do if something like that happens to you."

INSTRUCTION

1. "When we have a disagreement or a conflict with a person, we can behave in different ways. We can be:" (write the following terms on the board)

   - "Passive. This means we don't do anything about the conflict even if someone is treating us unfairly. We don't feel like saying anything. We might not look at the person. We might whine or walk away. If somebody found my money and I was passive, I might not even ask for money that I thought was mine."

   - "Angry. This means we are so upset that we might hurt others with our words or our actions. We might feel hot or tense, or feel like yelling, hitting or even crying. If someone found my money and I was angry, I might want to scream at the person to give me my money back."

   - "Assertive. This means standing up for yourself in a respectful way. You don't hurt anyone. You use 'I messages' and say what you want. If someone found my money and I was assertive, I might say, 'I think you may have found my lunch money and I would like it back.'"

2. "Let's use another situation to talk about the different ways we could behave when there is a problem. Pretend you are standing in the lunch line and someone pushes in front of you."

   - "You choose to let the person stay there without saying anything." Call on students to respond: "Which way did you behave? How do you know you are behaving passively? What might happen?"

   - "You push back. What kind of

behavior is that? How do you know you are behaving angrily? What might happen?"

- "You say, 'Please don't push in front of me. I would appreciate it if you would take your turn in line.' What kind of behavior is that? How do you know you are behaving assertively? What might happen?"

"Which kind of behavior do you think would work best to stop the conflict and help you to get along better? Why?"

3. Describe "assertive language" to students (list the points on the board):

- Stand tall, with head high and back straight.

- Look at the person directly while you talk.

- State calmly and firmly what you want and how you feel. Use "I messages." Don't make excuses.

- If you say "no," say it clearly and mean it.

- Don't be afraid to repeat yourself until you know the other person has heard you.

APPLICATION

Present the following scenarios and call on students to role-play them in front of the class, first passively, then angrily, then assertively.

- "You are watching your favorite TV show and your older brother or sister changes the channel."

- "The teacher asks you to stay after

school to help with a special project. If you stay, you will miss the bus."

- "Another student keeps trying to see the grade you received on a test."

CLOSURE

"When you disagree with somebody about something, you can choose how you want to behave. Which way to behave do you think is the best way to get along with people? (Elicit response: assertive) When you are being assertive, you are showing respect for others by asking for what you need in a caring way, and you are earning respect for yourself by being honest." ■

Follow-Up Activity

Form groups of three or four and give each group a copy of the "We Can Be Assertive" reproducible. Ask the groups to brainstorm ways to be assertive in each of the situations on the worksheet, keeping all the guidelines for "assertive language" in mind. Ask them to decide which solution they like best for each situation and write them down. (Younger students can draw a picture.) Call on each group to share their responses.

Home Study Activity

Intermediate: Give each student a copy of the "Being Assertive Word Puzzle" reproducible. Ask students to complete the activity, then use a dictionary to define any words they don't understand. Have a classwide discussion on the meaning of the words and how they relate to assertive behavior.

We Can Be Assertive

Describe how your group would respond assertively to each of these situations:

■ Someone went into your desk without permission.

Assertive Response: _____

_____

_____

_____

_____

_____

■ Something is stolen from class and you were blamed even though you didn't do it.

Assertive Response: _____

_____

_____

_____

_____

_____

■ You were picked last for the team and someone started teasing you.

Assertive Response: _____

_____

_____

_____

_____

_____

Being Assertive
Word Puzzle

P	S	S	P	E	A	K	A	I	E	V	A	D
C	H	R	O	P	A	S	S	I	V	E	N	I
O	A	A	I	L	G	E	S	T	V	P	G	S
N	K	S	F	V	Y	P	E	E	I	O	R	A
F	A	Y	I	E	X	P	R	E	S	S	Y	G
I	E	N	R	R	P	R	T	R	T	I	B	R
D	C	O	M	M	U	N	I	C	A	T	E	E
E	S	O	A	E	X	E	V	A	G	I	H	E
N	M	R	N	S	Z	K	E	L	Z	V	A	P
C	S	O	O	T	S	N	A	M	F	E	V	O
E	M	L	A	F	R	A	I	D	E	I	I	R
Z	U	E	V	P	R	O	B	L	E	M	O	M
W	S	M	C	O	N	F	L	I	C	T	R	M

FIND THESE WORDS:

PASSIVE	CONFLICT	EXPRESS	POSITIVE
ANGRY	BEHAVIOR	SPEAK	CONTROL
ASSERTIVE	AFRAID	FIRM	COMMUNICATE
PROBLEM	DISAGREE	CONFIDENCE	CALM

Lesson #18

LEARNING TO "STOP, THINK AND ACT"

Now I'll know what to do.

PRIMARY OUTCOME

Students will be able to use a specific technique to manage their anger to prevent escalation of a conflict.

MATERIALS NEEDED

Application: "Stop, Think and Act Problem-Solving Chart" reproducible, page 116

Follow-Up Activity: "Anger Thermometer" reproducible, page 117

ANTICIPATORY SET

Write the word "anger" in large letters on the board so that it looks big and furious. Draw a box around it with three "spokes" pointing downward and a question mark at the end of each spoke. "We know that we all get angry at times and that it is okay to feel angry. We also know that staying angry can lead to conflict and does not help us get along, so we are going to learn what to do when we get angry. (Note: As you teach each step of the instruction that follows, erase a question mark and write the appropriate word: "Stop," "Think," or "Act.")

INSTRUCTION

1. "The first thing to do when you feel angry is to stop. You might feel very upset, but you can be in charge of your body: calm yourself down, count if you have to, catch your breath, tell yourself you can do it."

2. "The second step to prevent a conflict from getting worse because you are angry is to think. Use your mind to review the facts: Ask yourself how you are feeling and what is the problem that is making you feel that way. Think about what you could do or say instead of just getting angrier. When you are feeling angry, when is the best time to stop and think?" Elicit response: sooner rather than later to prevent a situation from getting worse.

3. Describe again the scenario in Lesson #16 about the two students arguing over the ball. "Those students could have stopped and thought about what choices they had for ending their conflict. What do you think they could they have done to prevent their argument from getting worse?" Elicit and list on the board possible solutions: continue playing, take turns with the ball, see if there is an extra ball, agree to stop the game, play a different game.

4. "While you are still thinking about what choice to make, how do you decide if it is a good one? Ask yourself some questions. Will my

choice hurt me? Will it hurt someone else? Ask yourself what might happen as a result of your decision." Ask students to use these guidelines to evaluate the solutions on the list you wrote on the board (in Step #3), and then make a choice.

5. "After you stop and think, what do you do next? You act. Now you put your choice into action." On your list of possible solutions, read each item as if it were a choice and ask the class if they think the two students would be getting along better as a result of each choice that was made.

APPLICATION

Create a "Stop, Think and Act" poster that briefly outlines the technique. Hang the poster in the classroom so students can refer to it during this activity and in the future. Then give students the conflict scenarios that follow and ask them to complete the "Stop, Think and Act Problem-Solving Chart." (Note: Before students begin the activity, show them how to use the problem-solving chart by re-creating on the board the completed example on the next page.) Call on volunteers to share their answers. Point out that when students stop and think, they can come up with many good solutions for solving conflicts.

- You are working on an art project in a group. You are drawing with a marker but lay it down for a few seconds. Another person picks it up and begins to draw. You feel yourself getting angry. What do you do?

- You feel jealous because your friend was given the lead in a play. You are getting angry and feel like giving her a put-down to show her she's not so great. What do you do?

- You lost your homework on the way to school and the teacher gave you an "incomplete" grade. You are so angry you feel like crying because you tried hard to do a good job on the homework. What do you do?

CLOSURE

"When you become angry, do you think you would be able to use "stop, think and act" to help you solve the problem? Which do you think is the most important step?" Discuss if any one step can be used without the other. "They're all important, aren't they, in helping us figure out what to do when we feel angry?" ■

Follow-Up Activity

Give each student a copy of the "Anger Thermometer" chart. After they complete it, call on students to share their "anger temperatures," pointing out how the same situation can affect people differently. Say that when they are more aware of their own and others' anger, they will have a better chance to resolve the problem that is causing the anger.

Home Study Activity

Ask students to write a paper describing a situation in which they could have used the "stop, think and act" technique in a family or neighborhood conflict and how they might have used it. (Younger students can draw a picture.)

Example of completed "Stop, Think and Act
Problem-Solving Chart" for Application activity:

What is the problem/conflict?	STOP!	THINK. Three actions I could take:	Will this action hurt me?	Will this action hurt others?	Will this action resolve the problem?	ACT. What I will choose to do:
During recess two of us rush to the basketball court to play, but there's room for only one of us on the team.		1 I could push the other person aside and say "I got here first."	no	yes	no	I will suggest we play handball instead.
		2 I could suggest we toss a coin to see who plays in the game.	no	no	yes	
		3 I could suggest we play handball instead.	no	no	yes	

Stop, Think and Act
Problem-Solving Chart

Name _____

What is the problem/conflict?	STOP!	THINK. Three actions I could take:	Will this action hurt me?	Will this action hurt others?	Will this action resolve the problem?	ACT. What I will choose to do:
		1				
		2				
		3				

Name _____

Anger Thermometer

Take your "anger" temperature.

When someone calls you a name, how angry do you get? (Fill in the bulb up to the line that describes your anger.)

Boiling Mad

Really Angry

Upset

Annoyed

No Problem

What do you do?

_____
_____
_____

When someone pushes you, how angry do you get? (Fill in the bulb up to the line that describes your anger.)

Boiling Mad

Really Angry

Upset

Annoyed

No Problem

What do you do?

_____
_____
_____

What other things make you angry? _____

_____
_____
_____
_____

★ REMEMBER: When you become angry—whether you're boiling mad or just annoyed—**Stop** and **Think** before you **Act**. You have the power to manage your own anger so that you don't hurt others—and you don't hurt yourself.

Lesson #19

LEARNING NEGOTIATING SKILLS

We can work it out.

PRIMARY OUTCOME

Students will be able to demonstrate the process of negotiation for the purpose of reaching mutually satisfactory solutions to problems.

MATERIALS NEEDED

Anticipatory Set: Puppet, prop (such as a jar of paint)

ANTICIPATORY SET

Start an argument with a puppet (or an aide or colleague) that is holding a jar of paint. Teacher: "I need that color now. Please give it to me." Puppet: "No, I need it." Grab the jar from the puppet, then ask students, "Did somebody win that argument?" Elicit: Yes, you did. Puppet: "I have to finish my work and I need that color." Teacher: "No, I need it." The puppet grabs the jar back. Ask students, "Did somebody win that argument?" Elicit: Yes, the puppet did. "Did this disagreement end in a way that satisfied both people?" Elicit: No. "You are going to learn how both people can be satisfied when they want the same thing. You are now going to learn how to negotiate."

INSTRUCTION

1. Have older students look up the word "negotiate." Tell younger students, "'Negotiate' means to discuss something so you can reach an agreement. When you agree, it means both people are satisfied with what you decided to do."

2. "In this classroom, you have been learning a lot of new skills for getting along with one another." Review: treating each other with respect, listening, empathy, being assertive, 'I messages,' stop, think and act. All these skills will help you when you negotiate with another person to solve a problem."

3. "When there is a conflict between two people, it means that both people have the problem. When both people work together to solve the problem, they are negotiating. Here's what both of you do to negotiate (list the steps on a chart for further reference):

• "Each of you describe what you want. How would the people who wanted the jar of paint describe what they want?" Elicit responses: Teacher wanted to use the paint. Puppet wanted to use the paint.

• "Each of you give your reasons for wanting what you want and feeling as you do." Teacher: "I need the paint to color the flowers." Puppet: "I need the paint to finish my work."

• "Each of you describe how you feel. Don't keep your feelings inside. Use 'I messages.'" Continue with the "paint" example. Teacher: "I feel angry." Puppet: "I feel angry."

- "Each of you should offer plans for solving the problem. Listen to each other. You both might have some very good ideas." Teacher: "I could use a different color before I use this one." Puppet: "I could finish quickly and give the paint to you."

- "Decide on a plan to solve the problem. Be sure you both think the plan is fair." Teacher: "If you can finish soon, you could use the paint first." Puppet: "That would be good. It will just take me a minute to finish."

- "Show you have agreed. Shake hands, give a high-five or smile." Teacher and puppet shake hands. Puppet: "I'm glad we negotiated to solve this problem."

4. "Sometimes you have to compromise when you negotiate. That means that one or even both persons might have to give up something. I decided to give up using the paint right away because I thought it was a good idea to take turns with the paint. When you negotiate, you cooperate to find a solution both of you could agree on. When you negotiate and agree, nobody loses; you both win."

APPLICATION

To help students master the concept, model the negotiation process again to seek a solution to a different problem. (Use a colleague or coach a student volunteer to play the other part.) Then ask students to pair up and role-play negotiating one of the situations that follows. Tell them to think of

as many solutions as they can and agree on one to role-play. Call on volunteers to present their role-plays.

- Two people start an argument because they both want to use the computer during free time.

- One student in a group won't let another student play with them.

- A student heard that her (or his) best friend was gossiping about her (or him).

CLOSURE

"Negotiating is a very important skill to know when people disagree. When there are disagreements between countries, the governments negotiate with each other to find peaceful solutions to their problems. When you practiced negotiating, did you feel that you were working toward a peaceful solution?" Call on students to explain their responses. ■

Follow-Up Activity

Intermediate: Have students work in small groups to create a colorful "We Can Solve Our Problem Together" poster displaying the guidelines for negotiating. This activity will help them review and internalize the new information. Hang one of the posters in the classroom and the others in the common areas of the school.

Home Study Activity

Students can draw cartoons in three panels. First panel: Two people arguing. Second panel: Two people negotiating. Third panel: Two people showing that they have agreed on a solution.

CHAPTER 7

Standing Up to Bullying Behavior

Most adults have some memory of a classmate or an older student who bullied them or their friends. What school didn't have bullying behavior to contend with? But weren't the students who bullied just children who wanted extra attention—and got it by shoving other students around?

We may be tempted to think of bullying behavior as a problem that's always been with us and about which there's little that can be done. But nothing could be further from the truth.

Without doubt there were students who bullied when you were in school, but in our more violent society, bullying behavior is more frequent, more varied, and often more extreme today. Perhaps you had a teacher who believed that bullying was just a "stage" that some students go through, or that there was little he or she could do about the behavior of a few bad lots who bullied. Today we know more about why students bully, what types of behavior constitute bullying, how to effectively protect the victims of bullies, and how to help students stop bullying others.

Bullying is not just a fact of life—and you are key to stopping it. Research over the last 20 years shows that adult authority is the single biggest check against bullying behavior. Schools that are "bully proof" contain teachers who know how to recognize bullying and how to safeguard their students against it.

Being the victim of bullying behavior is a hellish experience. Remember, every day, there are 160,000 children across America who don't come to school because they are afraid that someone will bully them. Don't let that number include students in your own classroom. Use the information, lessons, and strategies that follow to help every student acquire the confidence and know-how to stand up to bullying behavior.

Understanding Bullying Behavior

What images come to mind when you hear the words *bullying behavior?*

We tend to work from stereotypes when we talk about bullying behavior, and many of these stereotypes are wrong. Students who bully are not always big guys picking on small guys. Students who bully are not always underachievers picking on "nerdy" overachievers. Bullying behavior isn't always physical. And bullying is not just a stage that some children go through.

To help students stand up to bullying behavior, and to help children who bully change their behavior, we need to recognize what bullying looks like. We need to know what makes bullying different from typical aggression between students.

What Is Bullying Behavior?

As we've said, conflict between children is natural. Despite all our efforts to help students learn to get along, they will argue. They will fight. Sometimes their conflicts will erupt into physical confrontations.

But as long as you perceive a relative balance of power—both students are about the same size, neither seems intimidated, both are emotionally upset—you're seeing conflict on a fairly even playing field.

By contrast, bullying behavior is all about power and control. Here's what to watch for:

- **A significant imbalance of power—** students who are much stronger physically, emotionally, or intellectually victimizing weaker children.

- **An unequal level of emotion.** The victim is extremely upset—usually crying and often nearly hysterical—while the student who bullied is perfectly calm. He or she may even question what all the fuss is about. Such comments as "I didn't do anything," or "What's the big deal?" are common.

- **A pattern of repeated verbal or physical abuse** by one student or a group of students upon an individual student or a group of students. Bullying isn't about students who just don't get along. Bullying is deliberate and systematic. Students who bully target their victims and badger them over and over again.

Who Uses Bullying Behavior?

What does research tell us about students who bully others? First and foremost, it tells us to abandon our preconceived notions.

Students who bully are *not* always:

- boys.
- big in size.
- low-achieving.

- insecure.
- friendless.

Students who bully may be:

- girls.
- small in stature.
- of average intelligence.
- self-confident.
- students with friends.

Students who bully display a personality type. They:

- **crave power.** Students who bully enjoy controlling and dominating other children.

- **lack empathy for others.** Students who bully have no feelings for their victims or concern for their victims' feelings.

- **lack guilt.** Students who bully show no remorse. In fact, they actually believe that a victim deserves to be picked on. They will justify their behavior with such statements as: "He's a wimp, and that's what happens to wimps."

- **have to get what they want.** Rules or ideas of fair play are inconsequential to students who bully. They have to win the game or be the first in line—and if someone else doesn't like it or gets in their way, that's tough.

Four Types of Bullying

Students who bully don't just beat up other students. Bullying behavior is more pervasive and more subtle than that. Researchers identify four types:

- Physical aggression.
- Social alienation.
- Verbal aggression.
- Intimidation.

Generally, boys who bully tend to be more aggressive and more physical and girls tend to bully with social alienation and intimidation techniques. Within each category, the specific behaviors can escalate from mild to severe.

Physical aggression: Initially, bullying behaviors are limited to pushing, shoving, or spitting. If those actions don't achieve the desired outcome—which may be to get an object or a particular reaction from their victim—students who bully move on to kicking and hitting. As the bullying continues, they may get into acts that are physically humiliating, such as pulling down the victim's pants. They may lock the victim in a closed area. The most severe behavior is to try to seriously hurt the victim or to threaten with a weapon.

Social alienation: The behavior starts with gossip about the victim and embarrassing statements made to the child. Students who bully may call their victim names, use ethnic slurs, and spread false rumors about the child. This behavior escalates to social rejection. They'll use their power over other children to isolate the child: "Don't talk to her," or "None of us is going to play with her."

Verbal aggression: This starts with name calling and taunting. It escalates into teasing about appearance, possessions, family background, and so on. As it gets more serious, students who bully relay verbal threats of violence or physical harm: "I'm gonna get you after school."

Intimidation: Students who bully may first threaten to reveal personal information that would be embarrassing to the victim: "I'm gonna tell everyone. . ." Or, they may dare their victim to do something—such as stealing—that they know could get the child into trouble. Intimidation may be also begin by defacing a victim's property—clothing, bicycle, sports equipment—or playing dirty tricks on the child. As the intimidation escalates, they'll extort the child's possessions, such as toys, lunch money, and clothing.

Identifying Victims of Bullying Behavior

When we consider the wide range of behaviors that constitutes bullying, we can begin to see why bullying is such a pervasive problem today. A huge number of students are on the receiving end of bullying behaviors by peers. But research shows that there are also certain children who are more likely than others to be targeted by students who bully. They include two general types: passive victims and provocative victims.

Broadly speaking, *passive victims* are students who are unable to stick up for themselves and who give in quickly when threatened. They include children with these characteristics:

- **Loners:** Students who are often by themselves and not part of a group, especially at lunch and recess.

- **Physically weak children:** Students who can't defend themselves when confronted.

- **Children who cry easily.** These children are targeted by students who bully because it's easy to feel power over someone reduced to tears.

- **Children with very weak social skills.** These students are often anxious, insecure, and easily intimidated.

- **Children who have learning problems.** Any student who is "different" because of an intellectual or emotional handicap has a higher probability of being the victim of bullying behavior.

At first glance, *provocative victims* may seem to "ask for it." Many are children who suffer from Attention Deficit Disorder (ADD). They:

- **Are often restless, impulsive, and unfocused.**

- **Have poor social skills.**

- **Tease others and pick fights.**

As the term *provocative* implies, provocative victims tend to provoke others. They are not passive children, and that makes confrontations between students who bully and provocative victims harder to spot. These students may start an argument. If picked on, they will fight back. But keep in mind that notion of a "balance of power" in conflicts. Even when they instigate the confrontation, these children are not in a fair fight. Students who bully may be physically, emotionally, or intellectually stronger than the provocative victim.

On pages 129 and 133 you'll find ★ *Lessons #21 and #22: Dealing with Bullying Behavior*. These lessons are designed to help students learn how to identify and respond effectively to bullying behavior. As you teach these techniques to your class, pay special attention to those children whose personalities or physical qualities put them at special risk. Devote extra time to working with these students and helping them learn how to avoid situations where they may be victimized, how to stand up to bullying behavior, and—perhaps most important—to recognize that it's okay to ask for help from adults or friends. Children often feel it's a sign of weakness to seek assistance when they're the target of bullying behavior. You need to convince these students that it's just plain smart!

Preventing Sexual Harassment Between Students

Sexual harassment is generally defined as any unwelcome conduct—touches, comments, or acts of coercion—directed toward a person because of his or her gender. Most adults today are more aware of the problem of sexual harassment than ever before. As our personal awareness grows, so must our professional awareness. Sexual harassment is a type of bullying that can be found even in the elementary grades.

You may be surprised by that statement or all too familiar with the problem of sexual harassment. Reports show that sexually offensive language and behavior are on the increase in elementary schools—even among students in the lower grades. Conflicts between boys and girls often stem from sexual stereotyping and teasing.

Recognizing Sexual Harassment

Just as men are more likely to harass than women, boys are more likely to engage in sexual harassment than girls. Boys may also aim homophobic comments—such as calling names like "faggot"—toward other boys. But what's harassment and what's just teasing or flirting? Your first concern in dealing with sexual harassment may be in knowing when it's occurring. That's a common problem in all places where sexual harassment is an issue. Often it's a question of how the person who is on the receiving end of the comments or advances feels. Here's how a group of teens and preteens describe the difference between flirting and sexual harassment:

Flirting/Teasing	Sexual Harassment
feels good	feels bad
makes me feel attractive	makes me feel cheap
is a compliment	is degrading
is two way	is one way
feels positive	feels out of control
I liked it	makes me feel helpless

Clearly, in identifying cases of possible harassment, you need to talk with the student who is the object of the comments or actions. How the girl or boy feels about the attention will be the best indicator of whether the conduct is harmless teasing or flirting or true harassment.

Preventing Sexual Harassment

Like other types of bullying behaviors, sexual harassment is about power and control. The harasser uses sexual language or gestures to try to humiliate and dominate his or her victim.

What can you do to prevent students from being sexually harassed in your classroom? Here are tips that can help.

- **Recognize that sexual harassment can be a problem at the elementary level.** Remember that adult authority is a powerful means of checking bullying behavior of all kinds. If we refuse to acknowledge that even young children can use sex as a weapon against others, we inadvertently allow such problems to occur. Watch and listen for inappropriate comments and behaviors and don't dismiss girls or boys who complain about a classmate's sexually aggressive language or actions.

- **Create a classroom atmosphere that promotes the dignity and respect of every student.** Many of the lessons for teaching prosocial skills and expectations will help in setting this tone.

- **Model by your own actions that you treat boys and girls the same.** Studies show that teachers tend to pay more attention to boys in class and to tolerate more boisterous or aggressive behavior from boys than girls. Aside from the educational implications of such discrimination against girls, we send the message that there are different behavior standards for boys and girls. "Boys will be boys" is not an excuse for sexual harassment.

- **Teach students to seek help from an adult.** This can be difficult for students to do because recounting what a classmate said or did of a sexual nature can be very embarrassing. As with other types of sexual abuse, a child may be threatened by the harasser not to tell. Respect a student's need for confidentiality in such situations and draw on the trust and rapport you establish with all students to overcome shyness or fear.

Obviously, the topic of sexual harassment in elementary school is a very complex one, and we can only skim the surface of this difficult subject. If sexual harassment is a particular problem in your school, consider a curriculum that focuses exclusively on preventing sexual harassment.

Helping Students Who Bully

The good news from research is that clear "no bullying" messages and teaching students how to stand up for themselves and others can create a safer environment for all children. But what about the students who bully? What can you do to change their behavior?

If teaching all students to get along takes time and patience, helping students who bully to acquire those skills takes a lot more time and a lot more patience. But unchecked, many students who bully are in a cycle of violence and antisocial behavior that will only increase in the future. Consider these research findings [Garrity, et al. 1994]:

- Of boys who demonstrated bullying behaviors in second grade, 60 percent were convicted of a felony by age 24.

- The more aggressive a boy is at age 8, the

more likely he is as an adult to not finish college, to not find or hold a job, and to be in trouble with the law.

- Girls who bully are more likely as mothers to use aggressive means of punishing their children, who, in turn, are more likely to bully and abuse others.

Changing the Bullying Behavior

We said earlier that students who bully display a personality type. To help these students, teachers need to strengthen certain skills and feelings that are weak or lacking in these children. For example, work to help them:

- Increase their awareness of others' feelings.
- Increase their ability to empathize with others.
- Manage their anger in appropriate ways.
- Find alternatives to aggression in solving problems.
- Learn to be responsible and accountable for their actions.

Although the lessons in this book have not been written specifically for helping students who bully, many can assist in improving their behavior. For lessons that focus on the behaviors identified above, return to the following:

- Treating Each Other with Respect, page 27.
- Understanding Our Feelings, page 53.
- Displaying Empathy, page 63.
- Learning to Stop, Think and Act, page 113.
- Learning Negotiating Skills, page 119.

Other strategies you can use with students who display bullying behavior are:

- Pairing consequences for inappropriate behavior with an activity that teaches students prosocial alternatives, such as writing a paper about a person who is known for altruistic behavior, such as Mahatma Gandhi or Mother Teresa.
- Having students counsel younger students with similar problems.
- Having students set specific weekly goals regarding positive interactions with peers.
- Having students keep personal journals in which they can express their anger, air frustrations and concerns, and ask for advice regarding peer interactions.

As you work with students who bully, look for opportunities to praise them for positive, appropriate behavior. However, a word of caution here. These students often operate from a mindset that's very different from other children. They may interpret excessive praise as meaning they've pulled the wool over your eyes. Be very specific in your praise and only praise when a student genuinely deserves it.

In fact, because intervening to help students who bully can be so time consuming and taxing for a classroom teacher, you may need to refer these students to a trained counselor in your school. If bullying is a significant problem at all levels, enlist colleagues' support in lobbying for a formal, structured, schoolwide approach to individual or group intervention.

Try Reading, Writing, and Assertiveness!

I suspect that many of the problems I see with my fourth-graders are ones other teachers can identify with. Because children are bombarded by violence, they have a very hard time distinguishing between what are appropriate ways of getting along together and what are not. I see a lot of physical and verbal lashing out at others—generally, a lot of aggression.

Consequently, I've concentrated on helping students recognize the behaviors that characterize a passive, aggressive (angry), or assertive response to conflict, and why the assertive is best. These aren't easy concepts for fourth graders.

Initially, I've found that my students have trouble understanding the difference between an assertive and an aggressive response. The "assertive" response doesn't look very different from an aggressive one! So we spend a lot of time talking about how the behaviors are different, how they create different feelings in others and lead to different outcomes. In doing so, I look for ways to develop students' assertiveness skills while reinforcing reading and writing skills, too.

For example, we read together the book *The Mouse, the Monster, and Me* by Pat Palmer. Each character illustrates a response style, and we talk about what makes the mouse's behavior passive, the monster's aggressive and how an assertive response is different and better for each of us (the "Me" in the title). We also identify characters who are assertive or aggressive in the literature we read and how angry words or actions lead to trouble for the aggressive characters, while assertive behavior solves problems for others.

As a vocabulary exercise, I ask the class to brainstorm for words that relate to each of the three types of behaviors: passive (*shy, timid*), aggressive (*bully, mean*), and assertive (*kind, honest, respectful*). We discuss colors that symbolize each type of behavior, such as red for an aggressive response, blue for a passive one, and green for an assertive response. Displaying the words and colors gives students an anchor, something concrete they can associate with each response.

Teaching prosocial skills as part of my curriculum has certainly made a difference in my classroom. Students are more cooperative and they get along better. They use their assertive skills when they have a conflict. And since we keep reinforcing these skills through reading and writing activities, they get constant reminders of what it means to be assertive if they should forget.

Jane Zophy, Mississippi Creative Arts Magnet School
St. Paul, Minnesota

Lesson #20

DEALING WITH BULLYING BEHAVIOR

Part One: Identifying Bullying Behavior

People who bully hurt others.

PRIMARY OUTCOME

Students will be able to describe the characteristics of bullying behavior and determine if they have displayed bullying behavior or have been a victim of it.

MATERIALS NEEDED

Application: "Bullying Is a Problem" reproducible, page 131

ANTICIPATORY SET

"Do you all remember the story, 'The Wizard of Oz'? Think about the wicked witch in the story and how she kept trying to stop Dorothy from going to the Emerald City. The witch tried to scare her and trick her and even harm her. That witch was trying to bully Dorothy. Well, the witch is make-believe, but there are real people who bully others. Bullying stops people from getting along together, so we're going to learn more about this problem today."

INSTRUCTION

1. Ask students to define "bullying." List their ideas on the board, then condense to a simpler definition: "Being continually and intentionally cruel to other people."

2. "Let's talk about what kinds of people bully others. People who bully can be girls or boys, they can be big or small, they can get good grades or poor grades, they may have friends or they may not have friends. People who bully usually want to have power over other people."

3. "How do people bully others? What do they do?" Guide students to come up with bullying behaviors and list them on the board: shove, hit, use a weapon, call names, taunt, threaten, harass, gossip, embarrass, spread rumors, reject, threaten to reveal personal information, dare, deface or take possessions, play tricks, threaten with a weapon. "People who bully don't do these things just once; they do them again and again."

4. "What kinds of people are bullied more easily than others? Who are the victims?" Again, guide students to give answers, and list them: people who are passive (don't stand up for themselves, quickly give in); people who are isolated (spend time alone, especially at lunch and on the playground); people who are physically weak (cannot defend themselves).

5. Ask students to share some of their own personal experiences and feelings regarding bullying behavior. Then ask, "How do you think it feels

to be bullied? Do we want anyone in our classroom community to feel that way? In this classroom, we have decided that we want to get along better, therefore we cannot allow any student to bully another. Would you agree?"

6. "You have learned that it is normal to have conflict, and that people can work out the problem together. People who bully, though, usually don't want to work out the problem and won't agree to do it. They want to keep power over other people. Later, we are going to be learning that there are some special things you can do if you are bothered by a person who is bullying you." *(Note: See Part Two of this lesson, "Responding to Bullying Behavior.)*

APPLICATION

Distribute a copy of the "Bullying Is a Problem" worksheet to each student. Have students complete the worksheet, then call on volunteers to share their responses with the class or in small groups.

CLOSURE

"Now that you understand about bullying, why do you think it is important that we do not allow this kind of behavior in our classroom?" Elicit responses: hurts others, doesn't show respect for others;

can't all get along together. Ask students to repeat chorally, "We will not tolerate bullying behavior in this classroom." ■

Follow-Up Activity

Have students read a story about a person who bullies. Ask them to identify the bullying behavior by writing a few paragraphs about the words and actions the person used, then to describe the behavior of the victim or victims. (For younger students, read a story and have them depict the behaviors in a drawing.)

Recommended Reading

Primary: Children's Television Resource and Education Center. "I Can't Believe I Said It," *Getting Along.* 1988.

Intermediate: Webster-Doyle, Terrence. "Boys Will Be Boys," pages 1–11, *Why Is Everybody Always Picking on Me.* Middlebury, Vermont: Atrium Society, 1991.

Home Study Activity

Ask students to bring to mind a movie or TV show in which a character displayed bullying behavior. Ask them to write two or three paragraphs (or draw a picture) describing the character's behavior and the victim's response.

Name _____

Bullying Is a Problem

1. Some ways that people bully each other are: _____
   _____
   _____
   _____

2. I have been bullied before by: _____
   _____

   This is what happened: _____
   _____
   _____

   This is how I felt: _____
   _____
   _____

3. Sometimes I have bullied my:
   brother. ☐ Yes ☐ No. If yes, because _____
   _____

   sister. ☐ Yes ☐ No. If yes, because _____
   _____

   friend. ☐ Yes ☐ No. If yes, because _____
   _____

   pet. ☐ Yes ☐ No. If yes, because _____
   _____

   When I was a bully to others, I felt: _____
   _____
   _____

Lesson #21

DEALING WITH BULLYING BEHAVIOR

Part Two: Responding to Bullying Behavior

Now I can handle bullying.

In order for a student to make a safe response to bullying behavior, the skills in this lesson must be practiced repeatedly. Students must learn how to judge the situation realistically and the teacher must support any student who needs help.

PRIMARY OUTCOME

Students will demonstrate the words and actions for each of three options for responding to bullying behavior.

MATERIALS NEEDED

None

ANTICIPATORY SET

"Let me tell you what I saw on the yard the other day. I saw a fifth-grader picking on a second-grader. The taunting and teasing just didn't stop. I realized that the fifth-grader was bullying, and that the second-grader was a victim. What do you think the second-grader could have done about the bullying?" Elicit responses.

INSTRUCTION

1. "Now that you know what bullying behavior is, let's talk about what you can do if you are a victim. You have three choices and you have to use very good judgment to decide which one to choose. The choices are: 1) Be assertive and stand up to the person, 2) Do nothing and walk away, 3) Get help." List the choices on the board. "We are going to discuss each choice."

2. "Be assertive and stand up to a person who bullies you." List the following steps on the board and describe them:

   • Stand tall. (Stand up straight with shoulders back and chin up. Stay calm.) Call on students to demonstrate this technique.

   • Use assertive language. (Use "I messages." Be firm and serious.) Call on students to respond in an assertive manner to the following situations: "A person is bullying you and. . .

   – . . . takes your ball away." ("I want my ball back.")

   – . . . pushes you." ("Don't push me. I don't like it when you push me.")

   – . . . keeps teasing you." ("Stop it. I don't like to be teased.")

3. "Ignore the bullying and walk away. This may take a lot of courage, but when you turn away, you show that you are very sure you do not want to get into a conflict with this person. When is a good time to walk away?"

Elicit responses: if you think you can't stop the bullying; if you think you might get hurt.

4. "Get help from the teacher. There may be times when it is difficult to stand up to bullying behavior or to ignore it. These are times when you feel that you can't stop the bullying or that you might get hurt. It is very important at those times to get help from a teacher or other adult you know and trust."

APPLICATION

Ask students to pair up and role-play a bullying situation. One person plays the person who bullies; the other the victim. The victim is to make one of the three response choices to bullying behavior. Then the partners are to switch roles. Monitor the students closely as they perform their role-plays. After they finish, call on students to explain what choice they made and why.

CLOSURE

"You have learned a lot about people who bully and about people who are the victims. If someone tried to bully you, would you know what to do?" Make sure everyone would know what to do, then say, "If you are ever in a bullying situation, will you all try to remember to make one of the choices we talked about?" ■

Follow-Up Activity

Conduct an art activity in which students in small groups make signs for the school that illustrate a ban on bullying behavior.

Example:

Home Study Activity

Ask students to write a story (or draw a picture) of one of the choices a person could make in response to bullying behavior.

CHAPTER 8

Creating a Caring Schoolwide Community

Throughout this book, we've focused on how you as an individual teacher can create a more caring classroom environment. Applied consistently, the lessons and strategies will make a significant difference in your students' attitudes and behaviors and in the spirit of camaraderie in your classroom. But as you well know, your students don't spend every minute of the school day with you. Many of the conflicts that erupt between students occur outside the classroom and away from your presence—on the bus, in the cafeteria, on the playground—in situations where students interact with children from other classrooms and are supervised by other adults.

To be most effective, the prosocial rules you set and the behaviors you teach in your classroom need to be echoed and reinforced schoolwide. Not only every teacher but every adult in the school—from playground supervisors and crossing guards, to cafeteria staff, to secretaries, bus drivers, and maintenance crew—should have the same high expectations for how students will treat one another. The caring community of learners you strive to create in your classroom will be strengthened when it's part of a larger community of learners in your school.

This chapter will guide you and your colleagues in building on your classroom successes in teaching students to get along to develop a schoolwide plan for promoting prosocial skills and behaviors.

Setting Prosocial Expectations Schoolwide

Obviously, it's not enough to just agree as a staff that you want a friendlier school. That's a nice sentiment that won't go far unless you put concerted effort into translating that goal into a set of concrete expectations that students can follow and adults can reinforce. Start by forming a committee of interested staff to focus on student behavior. Be sure the committee includes teachers, administrators, *and* support staff, to send the message that promoting prosocial behavior is every adult's business in your school. Here's an action plan to follow.

Assessing to Determine the Problems and Needs

Use the Student Survey on page 11 to get a picture of the kinds of problems students are having in getting along with children in other classes. Have every teacher survey his or her class. The student-behavior committee should review the questionnaires and collate the results. Note the problems students experience most often and the particular trouble spots, such as the cafeteria, playground, or buses. With that information, the committee can recommend measures—for example, better supervision on the playground or more staggered lunch hours to prevent overcrowding in the cafeteria.

Formulating a Mission Statement

Just as many schools develop educational mission statements to articulate their academic goals, a mission statement developed by the student-behavior committee that identifies your school's prosocial expectations can help to focus everyone's attention on this important goal.

The mission statement need not be long, but it should be clear and precise: *"This school will provide a safe, caring, violence-free environment where all students get along in a cooperative manner."*

Once the committee is comfortable with the wording, use the reproducible on page 145 to share the statement with every student, staff member, and parent in the school. Read it over the public-address system. Invite groups of students to print it on posters or large banners to hang in the hallways; ask all classes to illustrate a copy of the mission statement to display in their rooms. Post a copy of the mission statement near the main office, so that visitors are immediately aware of the kind of environment they'll find in your school. Include it in your school handbook and in other publications that go home to parents. By publicizing your mission statement, you'll demonstrate your intent to uphold it.

Creating Prosocial Expectations for the School

Next step for the student-behavior committee is to develop a set of prosocial expectations that will be enforced throughout the school. These expectations need not vary significantly from teachers' classroom expectations—in fact, the more consistency, the better. For example, schoolwide expectations might include the following:

- Treat others as you would want to be treated.
- No teasing.
- No put-downs.
- No bullying.
- Keep hands and feet to yourself.

Teaching Your Expectations

Inform every student, staff member, and parent of your prosocial expectations. Once again, invite groups of students to create posters illustrating the prosocial expectations to hang in the hallways, in the cafeteria, in the gym, and on the playground. See the reproducible on page 146 for a small-size version of the rules that you can distribute.

But equally important, you need to talk about these prosocial expectations with students. Introduce the expectations during the first week of school. In fact, you might plan a special assembly for the purpose of sharing the mission statement and the expectations. If possible, plan two assemblies, one for primary and one for intermediate students, so that you can use age-appropriate techniques—such as puppets with younger children and role-play with older students—to help students internalize what the expectations mean.

Reinforcing Prosocial Expectations Schoolwide

Just as in the classroom, you can't leave it at that. You need to continue to remind students and staff that your goal is to create a prosocial setting schoolwide. Rewards and other positives are the most inviting ways to keep your prosocial expectations front and center in everyone's mind. Your student-behavior committee is sure to think of plenty of ideas for prosocial rewards, but here are a few to get you started.

- Set up a **"Good Citizens" Honor Roll:** Each month, recognize students who are cited by staff or other students for consistently demonstrating helping behaviors. Announce the honor roll members over your public-address system and in the local newspaper. Help students and parents attach as much significance to making this honor roll as they do to an academic honor roll.

- **Start a "Caught Cooperating" Bulletin Board:** Set up a bulletin board near the main entrance or office. Invite all staff members—teachers, administrators, secretaries, cafeteria workers, bus drivers, maintenance workers—to add students' names to a weekly or monthly list of students "Caught Cooperating." Take an instant photo of each child to display near his or her name. Students are added to the list for special acts of kindness and cooperation in school or on the bus. Each Friday, share the names of students who were Caught Cooperating that week during the morning announcements. Send a letter to parents informing them of this important distinction their child has earned.

- **Buddy Up:** You know that there are many students in school who need extra attention and will act out to get it. To encourage prosocial behavior from these students, assign each an adult "buddy" or mentor who can provide that child with special consideration and guidance. While buddies may fill many roles depending on time and interest, the first job of each adult buddy is to keep an eye out for his or her charge throughout the school day and praise the student for helping behaviors.

On page 141, you'll find "Great Ideas: Schoolwide Campaigns to Reinforce Prosocial Skills." The three themes suggested make use of strong visual messages to impress students with your prosocial goals.

In addition, beginning on page 142 are a host of reproducible posters and awards to stimulate awareness and reward observance of your schoolwide prosocial expectations

Setting Consequences for Inappropriate Behavior

Once you've set your behavior guidelines and taught them to students, you'll expect them to follow the rules. So if students act out in the cafeteria or fight on the playground, they must know that those behaviors will not be tolerated.

Another important job of your student-behavior committee is to establish consequences for inappropriate behavior. Talk about them with students, post the consequences in the building, and include them in the school handbook, so that students, parents, and staff are well aware of them.

When setting consequences, always start with a warning. Give students a chance to change their behavior before facing a more severe consequence. For a second offense, students might lose a certain privilege for a period of time, such as not being able to go out on the playground, eat with their class in the cafeteria, or participate in after-school sports or music activities. Your consequences should work for your students, your staff, and the kinds of problems you see most frequently. But like classroom consequences, schoolwide consequences should never be physically or emotionally harmful. Consequences should be unpleasant but not unjust.

More Keys to Promoting Prosocial Behavior Schoolwide

Establishing, teaching, and reinforcing your prosocial expectations are three key steps toward promoting more positive behavior schoolwide. But they're really only the start. Here are other activities and strategies that are vital to ensure the success of your schoolwide efforts.

Getting Parents' Support

Notice that we've repeatedly recommended informing parents of your mission statement, prosocial expectations, and consequences. Like everything else that happens at school, you want parents' support for promoting prosocial behavior schoolwide. It may seem paradoxical, since in many cases it's the parents' lack of discipline at home that creates many of the behavior problems you see at school. But nevertheless, the more you can get parents to applaud your efforts and encourage their children to abide by your prosocial expectations—in the classroom and schoolwide—the more successful you'll be at creating a caring community of learners.

Monitoring Students' Behavior

Your prosocial expectations will be meaningless if they aren't enforced. And enforcement requires careful monitoring of students' behavior on the part of every adult in the school. If the results of your student assessment indicate a problem with verbal and physical fights on the playground and in the cafeteria, for example, then these areas are not being carefully monitored. It's not enough to have adults

present. On countless school visits we have watched yard monitors chatting together while the playground is reduced to a free-for-all. If the quality of the monitoring is below standard in your school, involve your student-behavior committee in spearheading a concerted effort to improve it.

As a staff, review the kinds of behaviors to watch for. As we discussed in the previous chapter, it's not only physical aggression—kicking, punching, shoving—that threatens students. Act quickly to reprimand students who call names, taunt, or use put-downs. Watch for signs that children are being socially alienated or intimidated by peers. Be alert to aggression on the part of girls as well as boys. The goal of careful monitoring of students' behavior is to stop conflicts before they reach a crisis level.

Every staff member should also watch for appropriate social interaction between students and reward it immediately. Students must feel that their behavior is noticed—both as a deterrent to inappropriate behavior and as an incentive to positive interactions.

Remember, too, the importance of adult authority in keeping bullying behaviors in check. When students know they're being observed, they're less likely to bully others.

Take a Group Approach to Helping Students Who Bully

In Chapter 7 we talked about the need to help students who bully. But the time and effort involved can be overwhelming for a classroom teacher who has 25 other students to consider. Recognizing this, many schools create group intervention programs that are run by a trained counselor.

There are advantages to a small-group format. Students who bully tend to blame others for their behavior; but in a group session, the members won't let others get away with that. They'll force a student who bullies to face up to his or her own actions. Weekly group meetings are also an efficient way to help several aggressive children at once and encourage students to learn from one another's thoughts and actions.

But a word of caution: Placing students who tend to be antisocial together can easily lead to disruptive behavior. That's why it's so important for a trained individual to lead these groups—someone who knows what to expect and can defuse confrontations quickly. Limit group size to no more than five students, to make it easier to manage the group and to ensure that each student gets individual attention.

Giving Students Helping Opportunities at School

An often overlooked component of teaching students how to get along is providing them with opportunities to display helping behaviors at school. Letting students shoulder age-appropriate responsibilities also gives them pride of ownership. It helps them feel a part of a team, a member of your school community.

What kind of jobs can students do? These are all tasks students take on successfully at many schools:

- Tutoring younger children.
- Reading to younger children.
- Performing for younger children, such as putting on plays and puppet shows.
- Being a buddy to new students.
- Helping in the library.

- Helping in the cafeteria.
- Assisting school secretaries with answering the phone and other office duties.
- Reading the morning announcements.
- Helping maintenance staff with jobs such as raising and lowering the school flag.
- Picking up litter from around the school.
- Escorting visitors around the school.
- Helping to resolve conflicts by acting as peer mediators.

Be sure to match a student's abilities with the task, to ensure the child experiences success. And don't automatically give these responsibilities only to the "good students." Sure, you want to reward students who consistently use prosocial skills and appropriate behavior. But entrusting a difficult student with an important job, such as raising or lowering the school flag each day, can do wonders for that child's attitude and self-esteem; in turn, you'll often see a significant improvement in behavior.

Educating Through a Staff-Development Workshop

To enable every staff member to acquire the skills and strategies to help students get along, lobby for a staff-development day or week—during the school year or over the summer—that focuses on student behavior. Use this time to review the lessons in this book and talk about the most effective ways to teach each one. Organize activities and discussions to help teachers and support personnel increase their awareness of the importance of setting prosocial expectations and teaching positive social skills, and their techniques for doing so.

Making the Choice to Change Students' Behavior

Perhaps the most important message for a teacher or a staff to take from this book is this: You *can* teach students to get along. These are skills that many students don't possess precisely because they haven't been taught them at home, where we expect children to learn the basic skills of positive human interaction.

Every day, you're presented with a choice. You can do something about students' antisocial behavior. You can decrease the level of conflict and aggression in your classroom and, working with your colleagues, in your school. When you choose to help students learn to cooperate, work as part of a team, listen, and empathize, you offer children skills that will have a profound influence on their future well-being. In the final analysis, there may be no more important skills that we can teach students than the ability to get along with others.

Schoolwide Campaigns to Reinforce Prosocial Skills

For students to maximize the concepts taught in this book, prosocial skills must be emphasized continually in all areas of the school and practiced repeatedly.

Promote and support the classroom lessons in this book that teach prosocial skills by scheduling a schoolwide campaign several times a year. Feature banners, bulletin boards, posters, displays and other activities highlighting important "getting along" concepts.

Involve students in the development and execution of the schoolwide plans by creating a staff/student board to discuss and carry out the activities.

Here are some ideas for your schoolwide campaigns.

DIVERSITY

Banner

"We Celebrate Each Other's Differences."

Schoolwide Bulletin Board

"We're All Different in Some Way." Classes submit photos or magazine cutouts that illustrate diversity (physical, cultural, ethnic, etc.).

Hallway Posters

Each class designs a poster depicting the differences between students in their classroom.

Classroom Posters

"Friends Come in All Shapes and Sizes. Make a New Friend." (See reproducible poster on page 152.)

Media Center

Students from different grade levels create a display highlighting literature from around the world.

Assembly

Have a special "festival of nations." Each grade level or classroom can choose a culture and share songs, a play, a dance, or a display.

COOPERATION

Banner

"We Cooperate Because We Care About Each Other."

Schoolwide Bulletin Board

"We Cooperate to Get Things Done." Intersperse photos and drawings of teams working together. Use captions to describe the tasks.

Hallway Posters

Each class creates a "We Did This Together" poster of their choice with every student contributing to and signing the artwork.

Classroom Posters

"It's Great to Cooperate." (See reproducible posters on pages 150 and 151.)

Media Center

Display group projects completed by students at different grade levels. List the names of the group participants.

Assembly

Each class learns the "Cooperating, Getting Along" song (see reproducible on page 92) and the whole school sings it together at an assembly.

GETTING ALONG WITH EACH OTHER

Banner

"We Know How to Get Along with Each Other."

Schoolwide Bulletin Board

"In a Safe and Caring School, We Get Along with Each Other." At an assembly, each class repeats the Classroom Pledge on page 29 and gives a signed copy to the principal. The pledges are glued together on a large posterboard, which is laminated and placed on a prominent hallway bulletin board or near the front door of the school.

Hallway Posters

Each class creates a poster showing how they get along with one another.

Classroom Posters

"We Have a Peaceful and Caring School." (See reproducible poster on page 149.)

Media Center

Have a display featuring books with themes regarding peace, safety and respect.

Assembly

Present "We Know How To Get Along with Each Other" skits in which each class contributes one or more role-plays showing both the wrong way and the right way to get along with each other. Celebrate all students' efforts at learning these skills by giving everyone bags of popcorn with this message inside: "In Our School, Getting Along Together is POPular!"

Posters and Positive Recognition Awards

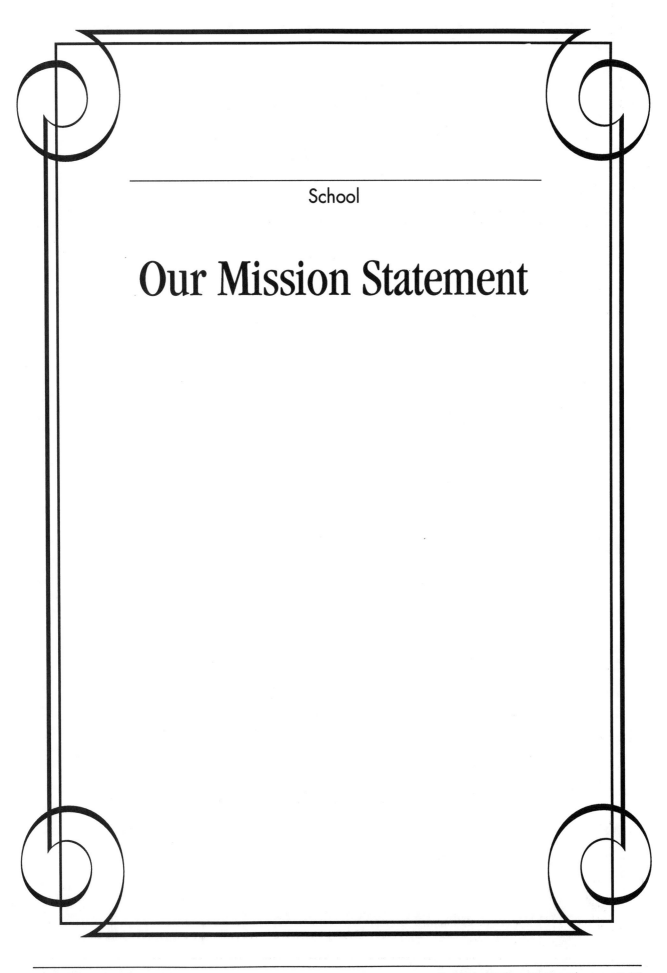

_____

School

Our Mission Statement

School

Rules for Getting Along Together in Our School

_____

School

Students' Bill of Rights

**All staff and students will make every effort
to observe the following.**

Students in our school have the right to:

- **Learn in a safe and peaceful environment.**

- **Know what behavior is expected of them at all times in every area of the school.**

- **Be protected from physical harm and verbal abuse.**

- **Have their positive behavior recognized.**

- **Have their personal property protected.**

- **Have their concerns heard.**

- **Be treated with kindness and caring.**

To: All Students

My Expectations of Students in Our School

I would like all of you to know what is expected of you as a student in our school.

- I expect you will represent our school in an outstanding manner.

- I expect you will work to the best of your ability.

- I expect you will treat others with dignity, worth and respect.

- I expect you will keep our campus beautiful and clean.

- I expect you will follow all the rules and regulations set forth by your teachers and the school.

- I expect you will work to keep a positive relationship with parents, teachers and friends.

- I expect you to reach beyond your grasp and learn new things.

- I expect you will make all of us very proud.

From: _____
Principal

We have a PEACEFUL and CARING school.

IT'S GREAT TO COOPERATE

IT'S GREAT TO COOPERATE

FRIENDS COME IN ALL SHAPES AND SIZES!

MAKE A NEW FRIEND

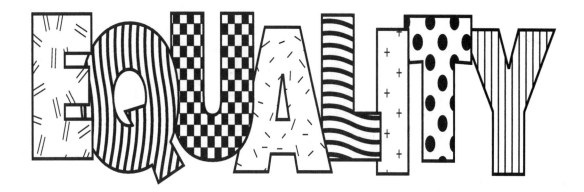

MEANS WE

ALL DESERVE

THE SAME RIGHTS.

MEANS TREATING
EVERYONE THE WAY
YOU WANT TO
BE TREATED.

MEANS WE ARE PROUD OF WHO WE ARE AND WHAT WE SAY AND DO.

MEANS STANDING UP FOR YOURSELF IN A RESPECTFUL WAY.

FIGHTING
Does Not Solve Problems.
TALKING
and
CARING
Does.

Be in CHARGE of Your Own BEHAVIOR

TEAMWORK

A Great Way to Get Along.

YOU SPARKLE
because you get along with others.

Presented to

_____

Signed _____

Date _____

For Blooming Good Behavior

Presented to

_____

Signed _____

Date _____

This class has real class.

Presented to

_____

for knowing how to get along together.

_____   _____
Signed   Date

_____
Class

is a
bunch that
knows how
to get along
together.

_____   _____
Signed   Date

Bibliography

Amherst H. Wilder Foundation. *Peace Is Not a Season, Peace Is a Way of Life!* St. Paul, Minnesota: Amherst H. Wilder Foundation. 1992.

Azok, S., Korb, K., and Leutenberg, E. *Seals Plus—Self-Esteem and Life Skills.* Beechwood, Ohio: Wellness Reproductions, 1992.

Baylor, B. *I'm In Charge of Celebrations.* New York: Charles Scribner's Sons, 1986.

Benard, B. "Fostering Resiliency in Kids," *Educational Leadership,* Vol. 51, No. 3, pp. 44-48, November 1993.

Berry, J. *Every Kid's Guide to Overcoming Prejudice and Discrimination.* Chicago, Illinois: Children's Press, 1987.

Berry, J. *Every Kid's Guide to Understanding Human Rights.* Chicago, Illinois: Children's Press, 1987.

Bickmore, K. *Alternatives to Violence: A Manual for Teaching Peacemaking to Youth and Adults.* Akron, Ohio: Peace GROWS, Inc., 1984.

Board of Education for the City of Londin. *A Curricular Resource Document for Violence Prevention.* Unpublished document, 1993.

Bodenhamer, G., Burger, M., Prutsman, P., and Stern, L. *The Friendly Classroom for a Small Planet: Children's Creative Response To Conflict Program.* Philadelphia, Pennsylvania: New Society Publishers, 1988.

Borba, M. and C. *Self-Esteem: A Classroom Affair.* San Francisco, California: Harper, 1978.

Brandenberg, A. *The Two of Them.* New York, New York: Mulberry Books, 1984.

Brown-Lehr, J., and Martin, C. *We're All At Risk—Inviting Learning for Everyone.* Minneapolis, Minnesota: Educational Media Corporation, 1992.

Canter, L. *The High-Performing Teacher.* Santa Monica, California: Lee Canter & Associates, 1994.

Cassady, M., and Sturkie, J. *Acting It Out Junior—Discussion Starters for 10-13 Year Olds.* San Jose, California: Resource Publications, Inc., 1992.

Charney, R. *Teaching Children to Care.* Greenfield, Minnesota: Northeast Foundation for Children, 1992.

Children's Television Resource and Education Center. "I Can't Believe I Said It," *Getting Along.* 1988.

Collins, R., and Hammond, M. *One World, One Earth: Educating Children for Social Responsibility.* Babriola Island, BC: New Society Publishers, 1993.

Crary, E. *Kids Can Cooperate: A Practical Guide to Teaching Problem Solving.* Seattle, Washington: Parenting Press, 1984.

Dinkmeyer, D., Dinkmeyer, Jr., D., and McKay, G. *Systematic Training for Effective Teaching.* Circle Pines, Minnesota: A.G.S., 1980.

Dorn, L. *Peace in the Family—A Workbook of Ideas and Actions.* New York, New York: Pantheon Books, 1983.

Drew, N. *Learning the Skills of Peacemaking: An Activity Guide for Elementary-Age Children on Communication, Cooperating, Resolving Conflict.* Rolling Hills Estates, California: Jalmar Press, 1987.

Edmonds, R.R. "Programs of School Improvement: An Overview." *Educational Leadership* 40, 3: pp 4-11, 1982.

Enloe, W., and Simon, K. *Linking Through Diversity: Practical Classroom Methods of Experiencing and Understanding Our Cultures.* Tucson, Arizona: Zephyr Press, 1993.

Friedman, A, and Schmidt, F. *Creative Conflict Solving for Kids.* Miami Beach, Florida: Grace Contrino Abrams Peace Education Foundation, Inc., 1991.

Friedman, A., and Schmidt, F. *Creative Conflict Solving for Kids*, *Grades 5-9.* Miami Beach, Florida: Grace Contrino Abrams Peace Education Foundation, Inc., 1985.

Garrity, C., Jens, K., Porter, W., Sager, N., and Camilli, C. *Bully-Proofing Your School.* Longmont, Colorado: Sopris West, 1994.

Glasser, W. *Schools Without Failure.* New York, New York: Harper & Row, 1969.

Goldstein, A., and Glick, B. *Agression Replacement Training.* Champaign, Illinois: Research Press, 1987.

Greenbaum, S., Turner, B., and Stephens, R. *Set Straight on Bullies.* Malibu, California: National School Safety Foundation, 1989.

Huggins, P. *Teaching Friendship Skills.* Longmont, Colorado: Sopris West, 1993.

Jackson, D., and Jackson, N., and Monroe, C. *Getting Along With Others—Teaching Social Effectiveness to Children.* Champaign, Illinois: Research Press, 1983.

Jackson, T. *Activities That Teach.* Red Rock Publishing, 1993.

Jaffe, P. *Zero Tolerance for Violence: A Challenge for All Schools and Communities.* Canadian School Boards Association Newsletter, March/April 1993, Vol. 8, No. 2, pp 1-2.

Johnson, D., and Johnson R. *Teaching Students to Be Peacemakers.* Edina, Minnesota: Interaction Press, 1991.

Johnson, D., and Johnson, R. *Circles of Learning.* Edina, Minnesota: Interaction Press, 1990.

Johnson, G., Kaufman, G., and Raphael, L. *Stick Up for Yourself.* Minneapolis, Minnesota: Free Spirit Publishing, 1991.

Johnson, G., Kaufman, G., and Raphael, L. *Stick Up for Yourself—Teacher's Guide.* Minneapolis, Minnesota: Free Spirit Publishing, 1991.

Judson, S., ed. *A Manual on Nonviolence and Children.* Philadelphia, Pennsylvania: New Society Publishers, 1984.

Kerr, R. *Positively!—Learning to Manage Negative Emotions.* Portland, Maine: J. Weston Walch, 1987.

Kreidler, W. *Creative Conflict Resolution: More Than 200 Activities for Keeping Peace in the Classroom K-6.* Glenview, Illinois: Scott, Foresman and Company, 1984.

Lavin, P. *Coping Strategies for Kids.* Minneapolis, Minnesota: Educational Media Corporation, 1993.

Lewis, B. *The Kid's Guide to Social Action: How to Solve the Social Problems You Choose—And Turn Creative Thinking Into Positive Action.* Minneapolis, Minnesota: Free Spirit Publishing, 1991.

McGinnis E., Goldstein, A. *Skillstreaming in Early Childhood*, Champaign, Illinois: Research Press, 1990.

McGinnis, K. *Education for a Just Society 7-12.* St. Louis, Missouri: The Institute for Peace and Justice, nd.

Minnesota Department of Education. *Promising Prevention Strategies: A Look At What Works.* February, 1992.

Myrick, R., and Wittmer, J. *The Teacher as Facilitator.* Minneapolis, Minnesota: Education Media Corporation, 1989.

Natale, J. "Roots of Violence," *American School Board Journal.* Alexandria, Virginia: National School Board Association, March, 1994

Office on Global Education. *Make a World of Difference: Creative Activities for Global Learning.* New York, New York: Friendship Press, 1990.

Olsen, L. "Mission: Imperative," *California Perspectives,* Fall, 1992.

Olweus, D. "Bully/Victim Problems Among School Children: Basic Facts And Effects of a School-Based Intervention Program," *The Development and Treatment of Childhood Aggression.* Hillsdale, New Jersey: Lawrence Erlbaum, 1991.

Peachey, J. *How to Teach Peace to Children.* Scottdale, Pennsylvania: Herald Press, 1981.

Peyser-Hazouri, S., and Smith-McLaughlin, M. *TLC—Tutoring, Leading, Cooperating Training Activities for Elementary School Students.* Minneapolis: Minnesota: Educational Media Corporation, 1992.

Renard, S. and S. *The Collaborative Process: Enhancing Self-Concepts Through K-6 Group Activities.* Minneapolis, Minnesota: Educational Media Corporation, 1993.

Schrumpf, F., Crawford, D., Usadel, C. *Peer Mediation*, Champaign, Illinois: Research Press, 1991.

Shure, M. *I Can Problem Solve—An Interpersonal Cognitive Problem-Solving Program, Intermediate Elementary Grades.* Champaign, Illinois: Research Press, 1992.

Shure, M. *I Can Problem Solve—An Interpersonal Cognitive Problem-Solving Program, Kindergarten and Primary Grades.* Champaign, Illinois: Research Press, 1992.

Sorenson, D. *Conflict Resolution and Mediation for Peer Helpers.* Minneapolis, Minnesota: Educational Media Corporation, 1992.

Thomson, B. "This Is Like That Martin Luther King Guy," *Young Children,* January 1993.

Wade, R. *Joining Hands: From Personal to Planetary Friendship in the Primary Classroom.* Tucson, Arizona: Zephyr Press, 1991.

Webster-Doyle, Terrence. "Boys Will Be Boys," pages 1–11, *Why Is Everybody Always Picking on Me.* Middlebury, Vermont: Atrium Society, 1991.